PHOTOGRAPHERS · ADVENTURERS · PIONEERS

THE AMAZING

KOLB BROTHERS

OF GRAND CANYON

ROGER NAYLOR

To my sister, Susan Mortensen—
because this is a story about siblings
and in that department,
no one is more blessed than I am.

—R.N.

Grand Canyon Association
P.O. Box 399, Grand Canyon, AZ 86023
(800) 858-2808 www.grandcanyon.org

© 2017 Grand Canyon Association
Text © 2017 Roger Naylor

No portion of this book may be reproduced in whole or in
part, by any means (with the exception of short quotes for the
purpose of review), without permission of the publisher.

Composed and Printed in the United States of America

FIRST EDITION

21 20 19 18   2 3 4 5

EDITOR: Faith Marcovecchio
DESIGN AND PHOTO RESEARCH: David Jenney Design

ISBN 978-1-934656-87-7

Library of Congress Cataloging-in-Publication Data pending

Founded in 1932, the Grand Canyon Association is
the National Park Service's official nonprofit partner,
providing private funding to enable Grand Canyon
National Park to raise the margin of excellence
for educational programs and preservation, build
innovation in park services, and support the necessities
not currently funded by federal dollars. The Grand
Canyon Association works to inspire people to protect
and enhance Grand Canyon National Park for present
and future generations. Proceeds from the sale of this
book directly support the mission of Grand Canyon
National Park.

CONTENTS

A leap in the interest of art. *Opposite:* Emery Kolb on the Tonto Platform, Grand Canyon.

INTRODUCTION

THE KOLB BROTHERS were rock-climbing, ledge-hopping, mule-chasing, river-running canyoneers. They were rash, nervy, and utterly fearless.

Ellsworth and Emery Kolb were daredevil adventurers drawn to the earth's most glorious wound. When they landed at the edge of the Grand Canyon, they knew they were home. The boys were equal parts artist and athlete, a dizzying combination that pushed them toward increasingly creative ways to risk their necks.

The Kolbs dangled from ropes, clung to sheer cliff walls by their fingertips, climbed virtually inaccessible summits, ran seemingly impassable white-water rapids, braved the elements, and ventured into unknown wilderness—all for the sake of a photo. Well, a photo and a thrill. Sometimes it was hard to tell which was more important.

Edward and Ella Kolb.

Emery Kolb at Rust Camp, now Phantom Ranch. *Opposite:* Emery Kolb photographing rapids in Cataract Canyon, 1911.

And they did it on their own terms. To call them innovators is a gross understatement. They carved out a way of life that didn't exist, essentially creating tourism photography on the cusp of the twentieth century. The Kolbs also became the first independent moviemakers. They produced the first reality show. They invented the selfie. They invented trail running and put white-water rafting on the map. Before there even was a National Park Service, they taught Americans how to explore their national parks.

The Kolbs documented their adventures and their lives, recording everything in photos and on film, just like much of society does today. They were ahead of their time. By a century!

Ellsworth Leonardson Kolb was born December 27, 1876, near Pittsburgh, Pennsylvania. He would be the first of four sons for Edward and Ella Kolb. Ellsworth would grow up to be an easygoing and rakish rambler. He was nicknamed Ed. Emery Clifford Kolb came along five years later, on February 15, 1881. More intense and combative than his brother, Emery didn't have a nickname but was likely called all sorts of things by the folks he riled.

By 1902, the brothers resided at the Grand Canyon. They were early pioneers, arriving about the time most prospectors had abandoned the idea of reaping mineral riches from the chasm, and were instead eyeing the fledgling tourism industry. The Kolbs set out to make a living with their photography, even though everyone they encountered—the government, the railroad, and a tourism empire—tried to stop them.

The Kolb brothers always liked a little drama in their photos. *Opposite:* The Kolbs became known for their river running exploits and adventures in the Grand Canyon backcountry.

The Kolbs were groundbreaking photographers, capturing a blend of epic landscapes and intimate portraits under primitive conditions. Their earliest darkroom was a blanket hung over a prospector's hole. Water was obtained first from a muddy cow tank several miles distant and later from the springs at Indian Garden, which involved a nine-mile grueling sprint deep into, and then out of, the canyon's depths.

But it was their astonishing journey down the Green and Colorado Rivers in 1911–12 that made them famous. With virtually no boating experience, the brothers spent nearly four months in deep river canyons, navigating 365 large rapids and numerous smaller ones, and not only survived but shot a moving picture while doing so. That little film would go on to become the longest-running movie in history.

Ellsworth eventually left to chase other horizons, although he returned to the canyon for the occasional adventure. Emery stayed rooted on the rim, raising a family, taking photographs, and showing his movie until his death in 1976. He was the very last of the Grand Canyon pioneers.

Kolb Studio remains. The wood frame building, originally constructed by the two young novices in 1904 on an eyebrow ledge, affixed to the world's greatest erosional masterpiece, still hangs on. There's a lesson in tenacity there somewhere.

The original little two-story structure grew and sprawled and now cascades down the cliff face, a jaunty triumph, a sneer at everyone who tried to pry the Kolbs loose. This wooden aerie has hugged the high ramparts, enduring sun and storm, heat and cold, holding fast for every breath the canyon took for over a hundred years.

Now beautifully restored by the Grand Canyon Association and operated as a fund-raising retail outlet and exhibition space, Kolb Studio perches on the edge of a wilderness of towers and temples, pinnacles and promontories—a cathedral of light and stone and sky. It sits on the shore of an ocean of shadows and shapes. Clouds sweep the porch, and ravens swoop past the basement door. Clusters of stars peek in the windows each night, and the moon uses the roof for a footrest. And the simple rotation of the earth, the rising and setting of the sun, floods the studio with a crescendo of shimmering color, both eloquent and scandalous. Every day. Kolb Studio retains the entire Grand Canyon as an epic front yard.

Ellsworth and Emery may have been audacious and often foolhardy, but Great Muddy Colorado! They sure knew how to live.

As Emery displays here, an adventurous spirit was as essential as a camera to the Kolbs. *Opposite:* Their 1911–12 river trip brought the Kolbs a measure of fame, which they promoted at the studio.

On the Tanner Trail, looking northeast up the Colorado River. *Opposite:* A young Ellsworth Kolb.

CALL OF
THE CANYON

TORRENTS OF MUDDY WATER swept down the channel, tossing debris and clawing at the banks. The Kolb brothers were carried along on the deluge, hurled forward by choppy waves. Suddenly, their raft began to break apart. Neither brother could swim. If their lives flashed before their eyes, it didn't take long—Ellsworth was twelve and Emery, eight.

In May 1889, a ferocious rain lashed the Pennsylvania countryside. The same downpour that caused the Johnstown Flood turned the Allegheny River and its tributaries into raging torrents. Naturally, the boys built a makeshift raft from lumber scraps and launched into the floodwaters of the creek near their home. What could possibly go wrong?

As they approached the swollen river, their little raft began to splinter. Desperately, Emery stretched across the boards, holding one end

Of the brothers, Ellsworth was the most adventurous. *Opposite:* Posing at the mouth of Havasu Canyon, a gorge in the Grand Canyon that shelters a series of beautiful waterfalls.

with his hands and the other with his toes while Ellsworth paddled furiously for the shore. Somehow, they neglected to mention this adventure to their parents.

It would be their first taste of river running and near-death experiences. There would be plenty more to come.

YOUNG MEN GOING WEST

Their life's work began with Ellsworth Kolb's restless feet.

Even with all their opportunity and promise of steady employment, the steel mills of Pittsburgh couldn't hold him. At the turn of the twentieth century, frontiers ragged and raw still existed across the American West.

Ellsworth, who never saw a horizon that didn't seduce him, left home in 1900 with $2 in his pocket. He rambled westward, working as he went. He manned a snowplow on Pikes Peak, swung a pick and shovel on the roads of Yellowstone and Yosemite, and served as a carpenter's helper in San Francisco. He signed on with a freighter bound for China but before shipping out decided to take a peek at a savage hole in the ground somewhere in the Arizona Territory.

Ellsworth hired on with the Atchison, Topeka & Santa Fe Railway, known as the Santa Fe, so he could travel east to Williams, a town that lies sixty miles south of the Grand Canyon amid a forest of ponderosa pines. From there, nearly broke, he walked the tracks of the spur line to the canyon for fifty miles then finally flagged down a train. He paid the reduced fare and rode the cushions the rest of the way.

President Theodore Roosevelt was an early protector of the Grand Canyon.

UNCLE SAM STEPS IN

When the first Anglo settlers arrived at Grand Canyon, they were marching to the tune of manifest destiny. Laws such as the Homestead Act and the General Mining Law encouraged newcomers to grab and hold what they could. Canyon pioneers staked mining claims, secured water holes, built trails and roads, and established a very primitive foundation for the tourism industry.

Yet a movement to protect the West's special places was also growing. The Forest Reserve Act allowed presidents to set aside important lands, and on February 20, 1893, Benjamin Harrison did just that, creating Grand Canyon Forest Reserve. Although it was a moderate level of protection—mining, grazing, and logging were still permitted—it marked the first government appearance at the canyon.

President Theodore Roosevelt stretched the limits of the Antiquities Act to designate Grand Canyon National Monument on January 11, 1908. With increased government control, rimside entrepreneurs struggled to survive. Early on, the Forest Service had worked well with canyon pioneers, but as visitors arrived in greater numbers the agency turned to the Santa Fe Railway to provide a more expansive and cohesive tourism infrastructure.

Aided by this government alliance, the railroad and its concession partner, the Fred Harvey Company, solidified its grip on the Grand Canyon, and one by one the pioneers went out of business. An angry Ralph Cameron, who staked out large swaths of land through shady mining claims, kept fighting, even after the canyon was declared a national park in 1919. But when the dust and the lawsuits settled, only John Verkamp, who ran a gift shop, and the Kolb brothers were left to compete with the Harvey Company.

The arrival of the railroad in 1901 opened Grand Canyon up to tourism. Here, Shriners, World War I veterans, and Legionnaires arrive at the canyon for an outing.

The Santa Fe ran the first train to the South Rim on September 17, 1901. Ellsworth Kolb got there just a few weeks later. Both arrivals would significantly impact Grand Canyon history.

Before the Atchison, Topeka & Santa Fe completed that spur line to the rim, the canyon could only be reached by horseback, wagon, or stagecoach. It was a grueling, kidney-pounding, dust-eating journey over rough roads, ensuring that travelers were hardy but few.

When Ellsworth arrived, the tourism trade was picking up. He quickly landed a job chopping wood at the Bright Angel Hotel, a frame structure surrounded by canvas tents. The hotel would later be replaced by Bright Angel Lodge and Cabins, designed by architect Mary Colter. Ellsworth soon moved up to porter, which paid better and included tips. When he wrote home, he regaled his younger brother with tales of the spectacular canyon. It intrigued Emery, who was manning a drill press for Westinghouse Electric Company but had begun pursuing photography as a hobby.

Five years, as well as a difference in personalities, separated the two Kolb boys. Emery was more practical, more cautious, and he tended to be more intense than the easygoing Ellsworth. Still, they were inseparable as kids, wading into a fair share of adventure and mischief.

Now with Ellsworth living on the edge of one of the world's greatest photo ops, it seemed only natural to pursue an artistic calling. Ellsworth suggested photographing trail parties as they rode into the canyon. The brothers plotted to open a photography studio at the Grand Canyon—until their parents threw a monkey wrench into those wide-eyed plans.

Edward and Ella Kolb refused to let Emery go gallivanting off across the country unless a job waited for him at the other end. Ellsworth vowed to find work for his sibling. A few months later, Ellsworth wrote to say the Hance Asbestos Mine had agreed to employ the younger Kolb and had even furnished $40 train fare as a show of good faith.

Fearless tourists posed for the Kolbs.
Left: Emery Kolb with his dog. *Opposite:* Never one to resist a daring pose, Ellsworth nonchalantly steps over the brink.

STARTING A BUSINESS

In October 1902, twenty-one-year-old Emery, carrying his camera, guitar, and mouth organ, followed his brother into the west. After a long journey by rail, with Emery entertaining his fellow passengers, he finally chugged into Williams. Before boarding the train to the canyon, he stopped at a photography store and studio to buy supplies. As it happened, the business was for sale.

It must have felt like one of those serendipitous moments in life. The fact that Emery had no money didn't dampen his enthusiasm. He proceeded to the canyon only to discover the mine had closed. Now without the thrilling career of asbestos mining in his future, photography definitely seemed the way to go.

The next day, Emery covered his brother's shift at the hotel while Ellsworth went to Williams to get some details. No harm in just talking, right? When he returned by the afternoon train, the Kolb brothers were in the photography business. Always impetuous, Ellsworth had bought the building and all the inventory for $425—which they didn't have—on the installment plan. It was more money, Emery said later, than he thought there was in the whole world.

But having a studio in Williams wasn't the same as having one on the edge of the abyss. The Kolbs wanted to open at the South Rim but were denied by the Forest Reserve ranger, who managed things before Grand Canyon became a national park.

Officials at the Forest Reserve saw the rising tourism potential and initiated an informal partnership with the Atchison, Topeka & Santa Fe Railway and the Fred Harvey Company,

Early twentieth-century Grand Canyon photography required carrying bulky equipment and heavy glass plates in rugged terrain. Here Emery balances precariously behind his tripod.

Pete Berry built the Grand View Hotel in the 1890s. *Right:* Ralph Cameron. *Below:* In exchange for the right to build a studio at the head of Bright Angel Trail, the Kolbs manned the tollgate, collecting fees for Ralph Cameron.

which operated hotels and restaurants at railroad stops. The Harvey Company didn't want competition from the Kolbs. This rejection was the opening salvo in what would become a long-running feud.

When the railroad built its depot near the Bright Angel Hotel, it effectively created the center for tourist activity at the canyon. This area would become known as Grand Canyon Village. As it continued to grow it left other independent operations like the Grand View Hotel to the east, operated by Pete Berry, and Bass Camp to the west, owned by William Bass, struggling to attract tourists.

Emery ran the Williams operation for a year, mostly photographing saloon girls. It wasn't the glamorous world of asbestos mining, but it was a living. At every opportunity, he and his brother explored the depths of the canyon. Their fortunes took another good turn thanks to the most controversial of all the Grand Canyon pioneers, Ralph Cameron.

Cameron arrived in the 1890s and filed mining claims on everything in sight. But he was only interested in what he could mine from tourists' pockets. Cameron helped construct the Bright Angel Trail and charged a toll for its use. He built a hotel on the rim and waged protracted legal battles against the government, the railroad, and the Fred Harvey Company. Cameron allowed the Kolbs to set up their studio on his claim at the head of the Bright

The Kolbs began their photography business with a tent studio near Ralph Cameron's hotel. *Bottom:* Guests on the porch of Ralph Cameron's hotel.

Angel. As part their agreement, the brothers would man the tollgate, collecting fees from anyone who used the Bright Angel Trail to access the inner canyon.

In the autumn of 1903, the brothers demolished their Williams studio and shipped the lumber to Cameron, who used it to build a barn. The Kolb boys moved to the South Rim and began their career as Grand Canyon photographers.

The men who would help revolutionize American travel photography started from extremely humble beginnings.

At first they slept on the ground. Their studio consisted of a simple tent cabin near Ralph Cameron's hotel. For a darkroom they threw a blanket over an old prospecting hole gouged from the canyon wall. The photographic process required several chemicals, glass plate negatives, and water to develop them. The latter was a problem in an arid landscape. Their most accessible source of water was a muddy cow pond eleven miles away.

Ralph Cameron was an early pioneer at Grand Canyon but fought to prevent it from becoming a national park.

GRAND CANYON'S FAVORITE SCOUNDREL

He was the man who carved out Bright Angel Trail, the preeminent route into the Grand Canyon, and welcomed the Kolbs. But his motives were not exactly pure. He built the path as a toll road and brought the brothers on board to collect the fees. He also filed claims at Indian Garden, a rest stop on the trail, so he could charge for water and for use of the outhouse.

Virtually all of his mining claims were bogus, simple land grabs lacking even a whiff of ore. Cameron fought every level of protection the government tried to cast over the canyon. When Theodore Roosevelt used the Antiquities Act to create Grand Canyon National Monument, Cameron battled it all the way to the U.S. Supreme Court, where he lost.

Cameron was elected as Arizona's territorial delegate to the U.S. House of Representatives in 1908, and he worked tirelessly for statehood. Just days after Cameron left office, Arizona became the forty-eighth state on February 14, 1912. It was the last of the contiguous states.

In 1920, Cameron returned to office when he won a seat in the U.S. Senate. Yet this time around he had no higher calling and focused solely on protecting his personal Grand Canyon interests. He filed lawsuits that dragged out for years and refused to comply when rulings went against him. He tried to defund the Department of the Interior, tried to have National Park Service director Stephen Mather removed, fought to regain control of Bright Angel Trail, and proposed building hydroelectric dams in the new national park. He was voted out of office after a single term. Cameron died in 1953 and is buried in the Grand Canyon Pioneer Cemetery.

RUNNING WITH THE MULES

The bulk of the Kolb brothers' business was photographing mule riders as they clip-clopped into the canyon and then selling them the prints when they returned to the rim. Just like that, the Kolbs created the instant souvenir photograph, long before the instant camera was even a pipe dream at Polaroid. The Kolbs would go on to photograph more than 50,000 mule strings descending the trail.

With their business growing, Emery and Ellsworth received permission from Cameron to add a more permanent structure. In 1904, they constructed a two-story wooden frame building that clung precariously to the canyon wall just below the rim. It looked like a gusty wind might sweep it over the edge.

The Kolbs enjoyed staging an occasional humorous photo. *Left:* Emery, Blanche, and Ellsworth on the back porch of Kolb Studio.

Theodore Roosevelt (front) and John Hance (on white horse), a famed Grand Canyon pioneer, explorer, and storyteller, start down the Bright Angel Trail. *Left:* Photographing mule riders in the canyon provided the bulk of the Kolbs' income. William Randolph Hearst is pictured at top.

Water was still an issue. Despite a thin veneer of greenery, the South Rim is parched terrain. Streams are virtually nonexistent, and porous rock layers quickly absorb the scant rain and snow that falls. To sustain the fledgling tourism trade, water was hauled in from Flagstaff, first by wagon and later by train. Since the railroad was not inclined to sell water to a couple of upstart photographers, the Kolbs had to get creative. They built a darkroom at Indian Garden, halfway down the Bright Angel Trail, and created a business plan that would make hardened athletes weep.

The mule trains would pause for a photo at the rim and then start down the trail, only to quickly be passed by the photographer himself. After snapping the photos, Emery or Ellsworth loaded the glass plates into their pack and sprinted into the abyss.

They hurtled down the switchbacks 4.6 miles to the clear spring at Indian Garden, where each plate had to be hand washed once, twice, three times. Repacking the plates, they turned and charged back toward the rim.

John Hance leads the William Jennings Bryan party down the Bright Angel Trail. *Left:* A prestigious mule party including John Muir (top), known as the "Father of the National Parks," naturalist John Burroughs (third from top), and journalist Ida Tarbell (second from bottom).

Ralph Cameron built a tourist camp at Indian Garden, deep in the canyon on the Tonto Platform.

THE OASIS OF INDIAN GARDEN

In such an arid landscape, a source of permanent water becomes a powerful lure, and that is probably why human activity at Indian Garden can be traced back 13,000 years. Archeological sites are perched on terraces overlooking the creek, most hinting at seasonal habitation. Granaries are tucked under ledges of the canyon wall.

Ancient cultures occupied both rims and often farmed arable lands near springs or other water sources. Later, tribes including the Havasupai continued the tradition, living at Indian Garden during the growing season. They planted crops of maize, squash, beans, and melons on the tablelands of the Tonto Platform and irrigated with water from the springs. The Havasupai built check dams and ditches to control flooding and increase their harvest. When prospectors arrived toward the end of the nineteenth century, evidence the land had been regularly farmed led to the name.

Ralph Cameron, his brother Niles, and friend Pete Berry filed mining claims on the site, but that was simply a ploy to gain control of the water. By 1903, tourists could spend the night at Cameron's Indian Garden Camp where tent cabins, meal service, and a telephone line to the rim welcomed guests. It was a picturesque spot, but over time, usage increased and maintenance declined.

Cameron, who served on the Coconino County Board of Supervisors, wielded enough political clout to hold on. The county assumed control of Bright Angel Trail in 1906 but leased it back to Cameron, who continued to operate it as a toll road, with the Kolbs as gatekeepers, until 1912. Even after Grand Canyon became a national park, Coconino County maintained control of the trail until 1928, when it was sold to the National Park Service.

This time, every step pointed uphill, always up, often in a snarling heat, passing the mules again, glass plates clattering as they ran, sweat stinging their eyes, regaining over 3,000 vertical feet. They would reach the studio in time to sell prints to the returning riders. This mini-marathon was often repeated twice—and occasionally three times—a day.

It took Emery an hour and five minutes to climb those cruel miles back to the rim, although he once did it in fifty-five minutes. That's ridiculously brisk.

Anyone who has hiked to Indian Garden and back in a day knows the exertion involved. It's a serious workout, starting with the steep descent that punishes knees and batters toes. Then the long slog back in the angry heat bites calf muscles and makes hamstrings moan. The switchbacks seem endless, as if they're multiplying somehow. And that's when you're doing it at a leisurely soak-up-the-sights pace, not outrunning a pack of mules. And then imagine turning around and doing it again in the afternoon. And sometimes yet again.

There are mules and then there are simply the mule-headed.

As business increased, the Kolbs built a developing room (lower right) on Ralph Cameron's claim at Indian Garden.

Two Harvey Girls use a "donkey telephone."

Blanche Kolb.
Opposite: Emery Kolb
tips his hat to the canyon.

VIEW STALKERS

BEAUTY APPEARED IN MANY FORMS around the Grand Canyon. While in Williams one afternoon, the boys spotted a lovely young lady stepping off the train. Emery immediately announced that there was the girl he was going to marry. If nothing else, Emery was a man of his word, and this bold proclamation proved it once again. Emery and Blanche Bender, the young woman who came west from Illinois, tied the knot on October 17, 1905.

The photography business slowly grew. Blanche operated the gift shop at the studio, and the brothers continued to explore more of the wonders of the canyon, documenting what they found.

FRED AND HIS GIRLS

Fred Harvey taught America to eat with a fork. Before trains included dining cars, a passenger's only option on long journeys out West was grabbing a hurried meal at a roadhouse near the train station, assuming there was time and assuming the food was even remotely edible, which was rare.

Harvey, an English immigrant, established a string of restaurants along the Santa Fe line starting in 1875 that featured fresh food on table linen and fine china sided with silverware. Best of all, meals were served by attractive, well-mannered young women known as Harvey Girls. More than just waitresses, Harvey Girls injected a sweet dose of civilization into frontier towns. Humorist Will Rogers said that Fred Harvey and his waitresses "kept the West supplied with food and wives."

Above: Harvey Girls in their evening uniforms with manager Victor Patrosso, circa 1926.

Havasu Falls. *Right:* Captain Billy Burro, a member of the Havasupai Tribe, strikes a pose for the Kolbs at Havasu Falls.

GRAND ADVENTURERS

They made the fifty-mile trek to Havasu Canyon in 1905 and again in 1908, photographing members of the Havasupai tribe and the many waterfalls cradled among those canyon walls, a wholly unexpected and utterly spectacular oasis.

In 1909, they decided to treat themselves to a vacation, so they traveled to the far eastern edge of the canyon where they located the abandoned Tanner Trail, a steep, sketchy route long neglected. From there the brothers dropped to the Beamer Trail, a stony tightrope in spots. They crossed high exposed ledges and navigated rockslides as they made their way to the Colorado River. After riding out a howling dust storm overnight, they proceeded to the junction with the Little Colorado River. Emery had been told a series of cataracts could be found fifteen miles upstream. Scrambling along the bank, dodging quicksand, wading in the water with cameras held aloft, and climbing canyon walls like spiders, they finally reached the cascades. They took the first-ever photos of the cataracts of the Little Colorado River gorge then turned around and made the long trek back home. Hard to believe the vacation went by so quickly.

Ellsworth's idea of a relaxing getaway: traversing the Hummingbird Trail.

A storm erupts over the North Rim, as viewed from the Bright Angel trailhead.

On another outing, they dropped over the rim onto the legendary Hummingbird Trail, which plunges down a sheer cliff face to reach an abandoned mine shaft. Dan Hogan filed on the Orphan Mine in 1893, a shaft dug directly into a 400-foot canyon wall. The Hummingbird Trail actually consisted of ropes, ladders, and chiseled toeholds. The photo of Ellsworth clinging to the canyon wall, with the abyss tugging at his back, the world falling away beneath him, is breath snatching.

That was part of the Kolbs' enduring legacy. They captured not just a landscape but a spirit. At the dawn of the twentieth century, when technological advancements seemed to be shrinking the country, the Kolbs showed America the frontier still existed—and they were living right on the raggedy edge. Wild places could be reached, but it took daring and nerve, and they were just the camera-slingers to pull it off. Their mule photos were mementos, but their canyon portraits were lusty dreamscapes.

The Kolbs inserted themselves into many of their photographs as markers to the scope and perils of the Grand Canyon. Sometimes they are there to provide a measure of scale, a human speck perched atop a towering ledge, a living comma pausing the viewer's eye at the base of precipitous cliffs. But often they emerged as characters in a larger drama. They appear clinging to cliff faces, climbing hand over hand on ropes stretched from treetops, and leaping across gaping chasms.

Their signature photograph is titled *View Hunters*. It perfectly captured that reckless audacity that would become their trademark. Ellsworth straddles a high crevasse with a slender tree trunk stretched across the gap. Far below him, Emery dangles in midair, clutching a rope with one hand and a camera in the other. He's angling for the impossible shot as Ellsworth holds the rope taut.

A decade later, when writing for *National Geographic* magazine, they explained that the dangerous method was needed to secure a photograph of the upper mile of Bright Angel Trail as it zigzags down the canyon wall. They described the steps required:

Two ropes are used; one tied to a log, the other given one turn around the log. The operator sits in a loop in this second rope and is lowered to a ledge below, from which point the desired view may be secured. Then he climbs the rope which is tied, and the second rope is pulled in as it becomes slack. Thus the operator can rest when he becomes tired. The ledge in this case was 55 feet below. Had anything happened, the drop would have been about 300 feet.

Emery straddles boulder cliffs above Stillwater Canyon. *Opposite:* The Kolbs would go to extreme lengths to get the photo they wanted.

They turned the image of *View Hunters* into postcards, and it graced the cover of the souvenir photo album they sold at the studio and through the mail. Even if a bit of staging was involved (it's unlikely the Bright Angel shot was taken using this method or from this location), we forgive the Kolbs because of the countless perils they faced in work and play. That came to define their artistic style—fearless and innovative. It's hard to imagine Ansel Adams hanging from a rope in a crevasse. Or Grand Canyon painter Thomas Moran inching across a cliff face with a brush in his teeth. The Kolbs were adventurers who just happened to carry cameras.

The baby and the burro: young Edith Kolb began her Grand Canyon exploration very early on.
Left: A young Edith Kolb poses for her proud father at Indian Garden.

DOWN TO THE RIVER

In June 1907, Blanche gave birth to a daughter. Edith Kolb was one of the first Anglo children born at the Grand Canyon. Edith also became one of the canyon's tiniest explorers. Long before car seats, proud papa Emery built burro seats—two box-like saddlebags that could be slung over a donkey's back. With baby Edith in one and the family pooch in the other, the family made many trips to the inner canyon.

The Grand Canyon is a land of ever-changing light and shadow. Photo taken from Hopi Point. *Right:* This PR photo of Emery (left) and Ellsworth (right) was used to sell their souvenir photo book.

SOUVENIRS

The Kolbs produced a beautiful souvenir photo book featuring a dozen of their classic images. Each album was bound in a heavy paper stock cover with a silk cord and placed in an envelope. These were big sellers at the studio, and for years the Kolbs contracted with the Albertype Company of New York to do the work.

The Harvey Company must have been impressed, because they culled images from their own photographers to create a remarkably similar book. They even used the Albertype Company and demanded an exclusive deal, mentioning the Kolbs by name in the contract. The New York printer quickly dumped the independent brothers in favor of the big corporation. Fortunately, the Kolbs signed an agreement with the Campbell Art Company, but there was no mistaking the intentions of the Harvey mob.

Emery and Ellsworth paddle the Colorado River with a burro in the canoe because…why not? *Opposite:* The Kolb brothers experimented with composite images like this one, which combines foreground rapids from one photograph with the background from another.

While happy to roam the backcountry, Ellsworth felt the river's powerful pull. His idea was to traverse the Green and Colorado Rivers, duplicating the journey first made by John Wesley Powell.

A one-armed Civil War veteran, Powell led a three-month river trip down the Green and Colorado in 1869 that was the first known passage by European Americans through the uncharted Grand Canyon. By the time Ellsworth pondered the adventure, only a handful of men had successfully navigated the route and several had died in the attempt.

The chance for a risk-filled, adrenaline-fueled adventure was all the provocation Ellsworth needed to dip his oars in muddy water. Always a bit more cautious and now a family man, Emery proved to be less keen on the notion of an epic river trip. But when they concocted the idea of using a newfangled motion picture camera to film the journey, the commercial possibilities were just too good to pass up.

There were, of course, a couple of tiny flaws in the scheme—most notably that they had virtually no river experience. Ellsworth couldn't keep both oars in the water at the same time. Emery had rowed a bit but never tangled with a major rapid. As an introductory course to the river, they were planning a journey of over 1,100 miles with a descent of 6,000 feet through unpopulated canyons filled with boat-eating rapids.

Yet as ill prepared as they were to face the raging waters, they had even less experience with motion picture cameras. Complicating the matter further, they couldn't even buy one.

The new machines were not readily available to the general public.

The Kolbs began searching for a camera in the spring of 1910, writing to manufacturers and sales outlets with no success. The Edison Manufacturing Company (yes, *that* Edison) wrote, "For Motion Picture cameras, we would advise you that these are only supplied for the manufacturer's use and further information concerning them may be obtained through the Motion Picture Patents Company N.Y.C."

Not until a year later did the Kolbs receive a ray of hope via a letter of May 7, 1911, from Frederick Monsen, a photographer and lecturer in New York City: "Since I last wrote you I have looked into the matter of cameras and can find absolutely nothing for sale or rent. Fact is cameras are picked up as soon as offered for sale as the Motion Trust people do not want any cameras on the market."

But Monsen sympathized with the Kolbs' plight and went on to describe two motion picture cameras he owned, a big Pathé and a smaller Urban Machine fitted with a Zeiss lens, both in perfect working condition. He offered to sell either one. The Kolbs bought the Pathé.

The brothers designed their own boats after helpful correspondence with Julius Stone,

Ellsworth displays the motion picture camera used to film their legendary river trip.

The boats for the Kolbs' river trip were built to order by the Racine Boat Company.

one of the few men to successfully navigate the canyons of the Colorado. The Stone party made the journey in 1909. When approached by the brothers with a few questions, Stone graciously offered information, boat blueprints, and government maps. The Kolbs made some modifications and placed an order with the Racine Boat Company.

While the boats were being built, Ellsworth traveled to New York to purchase the camera and other supplies. Ernest Kolb, nineteen, became the third Kolb brother to make the long train ride from Pennsylvania to the Grand Canyon. He, along with Blanche, would run the studio while Ellsworth and Emery were away.

All that remained was to locate another man for their party to help with the camp work. Several were interested but declined the position for one reason or another. At almost the last minute, they secured the services of James Fagen (also spelled Fagan or Fagin), a husky young lad of Irish descent with a beautiful baritone singing voice. Fagen made a very favorable first impression when he met the Kolbs in Green River, Wyoming, on the eve of the "Big Trip," as they had taken to calling it. He pledged his loyalty for the duration.

He would leave, weeping, three weeks later.

Before setting out on his quest, John Wesley Powell had no idea what dangers lurked at the bottom of Grand Canyon. Anything from plunging waterfalls to deadly river krakens seemed possible in those unexplored depths. Of course, that full-speed-ahead attitude only made his 1869 journey all the more astonishing.

If he had known what he faced, he might have chosen boats other than the heavy deep-draft Whitehalls. The big round-bottomed crafts were built for speed on flat water, with two oarsmen pulling downstream and a third man in the stern steering

John Wesley Powell's second expedition in Marble Canyon. Note Powell's armchair in the boat.

with a sweep oar. They were not so good in the shallow, rocky rapids of western rivers. Powell wisely portaged most major rapids. Then again, perhaps Powell wouldn't have changed a thing, because on his second expedition in 1871 he went with boats that were pretty much identical.

It wasn't until twenty years later that a trapper from Vernal, Utah, named Nathaniel Galloway turned white-water rafting on its head—or at least spun it completely around. Galloway designed a light flat-bottomed skiff turned up at the ends for ease of maneuverability. It could be rowed and portaged by one man. When faced with rapids, he swung his boat around so that he faced downstream while rowing upstream to slow his momentum and dodge obstacles.

The Kolbs would use the Galloway technique when attacking rapids. Their boats were also Galloway-style. The old trapper had designed the boats and led the 1909 expedition financed by Julius Stone. In fact, knowing the brothers were woefully inexperienced, Stone suggested the Kolbs hire Galloway for their journey.

But that wasn't the adventure they had in mind. Ellsworth later wrote, "But—we may as well be frank about it—we did not wish to be piloted through the Colorado by a guide. We wanted to make our own trip in our own way. If we failed, we would have no one but ourselves to blame; if we succeeded, we would have all the satisfaction that comes from original, personal exploration."

Sounds like a sentiment that could be applied to all their lives.

The start of the first Kolb brothers' expedition at Green River, Wyoming, September 8, 1911.
Opposite: Ellworth (left), Emery (center), and Bert Lauzon (right) with *Defiance*.

THE BIG, BIG TRIP

THEIR BOATS ARRIVED IN GREEN RIVER, Wyoming, at the beginning of September 1911, about the same time the brothers did. Then they cooled their heels for a few days, awaiting the arrival of additional supplies and James Fagen.

The boats were sixteen feet long, four feet wide, and flat-bottomed with a rocker. They were framed in white oak, with cedar planking overlapped at the edges in lapstrake style. Enclosed watertight spaces were formed by bulkheads both bow and stern. Each boat had two pairs of eight-foot-long ash oars.

When empty, the boats weighed 600 pounds, quite a handful for the lean Kolb boys. At five foot three, Emery weighed only 130 pounds but often exhibited a strength and quickness that surprised Ellsworth, who was half a head taller and went 170.

The Kolbs carried a month's provisions, camp supplies, darkroom tent, photographic plates and film, five cameras, and the big Pathé hand-cranked motion picture camera. The oars-

The Kolbs used a crude darkroom tent during their river trip. *Left:* Blanche and baby Edith.

man sat in the open cockpit, and the extra man rode on the deck behind.

Emery christened his boat *Edith*, after his daughter, and Ellsworth named his *Defiance*, because "nobody loves me."

They shoved off on the morning of September 8, filming the event and the gathered onlookers, who cheerfully predicted watery graves all around. If somehow successful, this would be just the eighth expedition to run Grand Canyon.

Before he left, Emery sought to ease Blanche's nerves with a flurry of letters discussing mundane details and never hinting at the danger ahead. On September 6 he wrote, "Now don't you worry about me one bit cause all our stuff is just right and at this stage of water it will be next to impossible to have any mishaps and even so it could only be a delay on our boats."

Ellsworth and Emery with the boats that saw them through their months on the river.

KOLB BROS PASSING RIVERTON UT GREEN RIVER WYOMING TO BRIGHT ANGEL ARIZONA.

The brothers enjoy a stretch of flat water on the Green River near Riverton, Utah.
Below: Lining the boats through treacherous Triplet Falls in Lodore Canyon.

The Green River flows almost directly south through open country for sixty-odd miles. It gave the Kolbs a chance to familiarize themselves with their equipment and enjoy Fagen's fine singing voice. The young assistant proved himself a good companion and hard worker.

Yet as they reached the canyons—Flaming Gorge, Horse-shoe, and Kingfisher were the first—with looming walls, fast water, and the jarring cannonball boom of falling rocks, Fagen became more morose and the songs tailed off.

THE RIVER'S JAWS

After crossing the broad valley of Browns Park, filled with golden hayfields and pastoral ranches (Emery carried on about the scenery here in letters to Blanche), the river began to slice

Navigating fast water in Lodore Canyon.

its deep defile, known as the Lodore Canyon, through the Uinta Mountains.

Everything up to this point had been a carefree jaunt compared to the pent-up fury in Lodore. Low water stripped away any semblance of civility the rapids might have possessed and exposed them as feral beasts, fanged with toothy boulders.

Even the sun abandoned them. Drenching rains fell during most of the eight days it took them to traverse the nineteen-mile

Still waters entering Flaming Gorge belied the challenging rapids that waited downstream on the Green River.

NEW CAREER OPTION

In Red Canyon, before reaching Browns Park, the party stopped at a ranch, seeking to buy provisions. The old rancher agreed, and the Kolbs walked to the house—only to discover it resembled an armory, with the walls covered in rifles and revolvers. The man's sons milled about, conspicuously armed. In return for the supplies, the man asked the Kolbs for help getting some horses across the river, having lost his boat in high water. The gather was made in a hidden valley, and the horses driven into the river ahead of the boat.

Once across, the rancher's tone turned suspicious and he demanded to know what they were really doing on the river in the middle of nowhere. Things got uncomfortable, and the boys were only too glad to put the ranch behind them. Farther downriver, at another settlement, the Kolbs discovered the distrustful rancher was a known outlaw who had served time for cattle rustling. He had more recently turned to stealing other livestock. It was then the Kolbs knew they had been inadvertently enlisted as horse thieves.

canyon. They navigated many rapids but portaged and lined boats through the most menacing, such as Disaster Falls—named by Powell in 1869 after it split one of his big boats in two—Triplet Falls, and Hell's Half Mile. Ellsworth was almost swept away, and both *Edith* and *Defiance* foundered, with water flooding the cockpits. Their long guns ended at the bottom of the river, and worse, they discovered their watertight hatches were not.

The gang at the Racine Boat Company got a hearty chewing out around the Lodore campfires. Some film was damaged, and sand and water choked the motion picture camera. It proved too much for Fagen, who went on frequent crying jags and awoke one night screaming, "There she goes over the rapids!"

Emery runs the chute between a jumble of boulders at Ashley Falls in Red Canyon.

Soon as they exited Lodore Canyon, they stopped at the first ranch to arrange transportation for their shattered assistant. The Chew family agreed to take him by wagon to the train station at Vernal, Utah.

The steady rains and added flow of the Yampa River, which joins the Green below Lodore, raised the water level and speeded up travel. The Kolbs made good time through the next several canyons, bounding through the rapids with plenty of thrills but no incidents. Long stretches of flat water gave them a workout on the oars. Word of their journey spread, and they were often hailed from the shore by local ranchers and treated to meals and gifts of fruit and canned goods.

The confluence of the Green and Grand Rivers formed the beginning of the Colorado River. (In 1921, the Grand River was

Cataract Canyon. *Below:* The boys portage a rock-choked section of river.

renamed the Colorado River, extending the Colorado into the state that bears the same name.) Even with their hard-won skill set, the brothers approached Cataract Canyon with trepidation. The canyon had so unnerved Powell and his men that they portaged every rapid. Since then, a number of men had entered Cataract Canyon never to be heard from again.

Ellsworth later wrote, "It is seldom the Colorado River gives up its dead. The heavy sands collect in the clothes and a body sinks much quicker than in ordinary water. Any object lodged on the bottom is soon covered with a sand-bar."

Still, the Kolbs met the challenge head on, and in fact ran all forty-five rapids in the forty-one-mile canyon in four days' time, which they thought might be some kind of record.

Scouting a rapid in Cataract Canyon.

After enjoying a long stretch of smooth water through Glen Canyon and a visit to Hite Ranch, the first sign of human habitation for 175 miles, the brothers arrived at Lees Ferry on November 6. Located near the confluence of the Colorado and Paria Rivers, Lees Ferry exists due to a happenstance of geology. The relentless line of soaring cliffs that characterize this landscape momentarily swoons. Sheer rock walls break apart, replaced by gently sloping hills. Lees Ferry provides a rare crossing point on the Colorado River.

Mormon leaders established a ferry at this remote outpost to offer transportation to pioneers traveling south from Utah into the Arizona Territory. John D. Lee was the first ferryman, settling here with at least two of his wives in 1872. For decades, people and animals were transported across the volatile river in small boats. It was ticklish business. Boats capsized and plenty of folks drowned, but it was the only game in town. Service continued until 1928. The next year, Navajo Bridge opened.

Lees Ferry also marks the beginning of Marble Canyon, gateway to the Grand and a return of turbulent waters. The Kolbs soon arrived at their first big challenge, savage Soap Creek Rapid, which had never been successfully run. Naturally, Ellsworth ran it.

Emery set up below the rapid, cranking the camera with Ellsworth's

A time-exposed image of Sockdolager Rapid in Grand Canyon. *Left:* Emery Kolb with a movie camera, Canyonlands National Park, Utah, 1921

At especially perilous rapids, one brother would often stand ready on shore with a rope and life preserver.

instructions to film any calamity that might occur, then to sprint to the bottom of the rapid with a rope and a life preserver. Ellsworth rode in high and hard on the right, skirting one big boulder, but when he grazed a second one the boat bucked like a bronco and flipped on its side. Ellsworth was hurled into the torrent but managed to cling to the gunwale. When the boat swung round and righted itself, he climbed back in and steered the flooded craft through.

Convinced he could do better, Ellsworth climbed into the *Edith* and tried again. But in the fast-falling darkness he missed his channel and hit a thrust of stone midstream that sent both boat and boatman airborne. The craft landed upside down and dumped Ellsworth, who came bobbing through the rapid only to be rescued by Emery in the *Defiance*.

"Somehow," Ellsworth would later write, "I had lost all desire to successfully navigate the Soap Creek Rapid."

As they traveled deeper into Marble Canyon, the walls soared higher, the gorge narrowed, and the river turned brutish. It seemed like every rapid was a churning maze of plunging drops, grasping whirlpools, and sadistic waves. And always the roar of the rapids echoed from the walls like a great liquid cannonade. Yet after only one portage they continued on, running the other rapids. Each brother had the river violently rip an oar from his hands, but they were recovered downstream.

Soon they passed the mouth of the Little Colorado River and entered Grand Canyon. They battled through monster white water, including Hance and Sockdolager Rapids, and kept cranking the movie camera. On the afternoon of November 16 they pulled into Rust's Camp (now Phantom Ranch) and lit a signal fire so family and friends in the village would know they were on their way.

The next morning they crossed the river, tied the boats, and stowed some gear in a mine shaft. They planned to resume the trip in a week or so. But as they hiked to the rim, a trail guide told them Blanche had been ill with appendicitis almost the entire time they were gone. She hadn't mentioned it in her letters, knowing Emery would abandon his trip. Emery and his family

The Kolbs' river journey allowed them to experience scenery witnessed by only a handful of men, like the towering walls of Marble Canyon. *Opposite:* The brothers spent part of November and December 1911 on a one-month layover from their epic river trip.

traveled by train to a hospital in Los Angeles. Emery stayed by Blanche's side while she recovered, leaving only when she finally shooed him back to the canyon.

A FRIGID NOEL

Over a month passed before the brothers could resume their river trip. A surge of winter weather dumped snow in the upper reaches of the canyon and chilled temperatures. They set out on December 19 with two passengers. Younger brother Ernest wanted to go—he was a Kolb, after all—but would travel only twenty miles to the Bass Trail.

Filling the role of assistant was Hubert "Bert" Lauzon, a twenty-five-year-old miner and cowboy. Having only recently arrived at the canyon, Bert worked for William Bass as a tour guide and roustabout. He would quickly prove to be a valuable asset. When some deceptively swift water flipped *Defiance*, Ernest struggled in the icy river until Lauzon fished him out by his neckerchief. Film ruined in the upset made dandy kindling for a quick fire.

Ernest left at the Bass Trail, so he missed the Christmas festivities. On December 24, havoc struck in Waltenberg Rapid. With the *Edith* snagged on rocks, the *Defiance* was pulled into a hole and flipped. When Emery saw his brother bobbing in the river and being battered by waves, he yanked the boat free and charged after him down the middle of the rapid. But moving fast, he failed to see a protruding rock that punched a hole in the side of his boat big enough to fit a person through.

Bert Lauzon joined the Kolbs for the second leg of their river journey. Lauzon would go on to work as a constable and later a park ranger at the Grand Canyon. *Opposite:* A winter storm over Grand Canyon.

On Christmas Day, 1911, Emery's boat emerged from Waltenberg Rapid, at river mile 112.

Top: Frigid temperatures and icy conditions hampered the second leg of the Kolbs' river trip.
Bottom: After 101 days on the river and countless dangers, the Kolb brothers arrived in Needles, California, on January 18, 1912.

Swift currents carried Ellsworth far downstream until, nearly paralyzed with exhaustion, he managed to crawl to shore. Lauzon stepped up once again, swimming out in the frigid river and rescuing the *Defiance*. Upon landing, Lauzon announced, "Young fellows, business is picking up!" Then he added, "And we're losing lots of good pictures."

Christmas Day was spent patching the *Edith*. It wasn't much farther downriver that Emery took a spill. A week since renewing their trip, and they'd already experienced three upsets and a smashed boat. But that was the end of their misfortune in the water.

Yet the bitter cold weather continued. Ice coated the rocks, making portages especially treacherous. They ran most of the rapids, lined boats through a couple, and were out of food by the time they rowed into Needles, California, on January 18, 1912, to a cheering crowd.

The Kolbs had spent 101 days on the river, traveling over 1,100 miles. They had run 365 major rapids and nearly twice as many small ones. They became the twenty-sixth and twenty-seventh men to row the Grand Canyon and live to tell the tale. And they were the first to record it in a motion picture.

ON TO THE SEA

There is no rest for a wanderer. In May of 1913, Ellsworth rode a westbound train toward the Pacific. Even as he contemplated an oceanside vacation, he was still mulling the notion of riding the Colorado River to its conclusion at the Gulf of California.

Ultimately, all it took was the first sight of the churning river to lure him back.

> We were beside the Colorado at last. I had a good view of the stream below, as we crossed the bridge—the Colorado in flood, muddy, turbulent, sweeping onward like an affrighted thing,—repulsive, yet with a fascination for me, born of an intimate acquaintance with the dangers of this stream. The river had called again! The heat was forgotten, the visions of the coast faded, for me the train could not reach Needles, ten miles up the river, quickly enough.

Once he arrived in Needles, Ellsworth roamed the streets in search of a boat. He finally located an Indian with a flat-bottomed boat built of pine that he bought for $18. He purchased a few meager provisions and launched into the swift-running water on the evening of May 23. He made a point not to learn what lay downstream so as to preserve the romance of the journey, although everyone he spoke to warned him that he would either die of sunstroke, drown in a flood, be shot by bandits or the *insurrectos* of Mexico's bloody revolution, or disappear in the swamps of the Colorado River delta. "It was all very alluring," wrote Ellsworth.

Carried along on the tempestuous waters, he reached Yuma in four days, landing at the infamous prison. After mingling with the locals, Ellsworth met a cowboy named Al Phillips who was anxious to go prospecting along the gulf. Ellsworth welcomed

Ellsworth completed the journey from Needles to the Gulf of California in 1913.

BURNING DOWN THE SKY

While piloting the river, Ellsworth observed a gaudy, glorious sunset, which is a common occurrence at the Grand. This is part of what he wrote in his book *Through the Grand Canyon from Wyoming to Mexico.*

A few fleecy clouds in the west partially obscured the sun until it neared the horizon, then a shaft of sunlight broke through once more, telegraphing its approach long before it reached us, the rays being visibly hurled through space like a javelin, or a lightning bolt, striking peak after peak so that one almost imagined they would hear the thunder roll. A yellow flame covered the western sky, to be succeeded in a few minutes by a crimson glow. The sharply defined colours of the different layers of rock had merged and softened, as the sun dropped from sight; purple shadows crept into the cavernous depths, while shafts of gold shot to the very tiptop of the peaks, or threw their shadows like silhouettes on the wall beyond.

him aboard, and the two men crossed into Mexico.

The current soon slowed as the river veined out in a series of willow-choked channels. They crossed Volcanic Lake, a wide re-collecting of the varied streams. They encountered smiling but armed smugglers, swarms of mosquitos, and rattlesnakes at every campsite until they touched the gulf. They rowed back on the tide several miles to reach Rancho Lo Bolso, where they caught a wagon ride to Yuma.

Ellsworth's was only the fourth voyage to travel from Green River, Wyoming, to the Gulf of California.

Ellsworth sailing in the Gulf of California.

Bert Lauzon waits on shore with rope in hand should rescue be needed.
Opposite: Emery Kolb on the rim with his Akeley 35mm motion picture camera.

A MOVIE FOR THE AGES

CHAPTER 4

WHEN THE KOLBS WALKED AWAY from the river, they were celebrities. Just surviving the harrowing journey was newsworthy, and the story landed in plenty of papers and magazines. The fact that they emerged with reels of moving pictures was truly remarkable and whetted the public's appetite to see more of the adventure.

The brothers hoped to debut the movie at the canyon, but their studio was too small and the Forest Service—under pressure from the Harvey Company—wouldn't allow them to use any of the buildings in the village to screen the film. What had been a testy relationship was about to become downright acrimonious.

So they took the show on the road. Before the word *multimedia* was invented, the Kolbs were putting it in play. The lectures were illustrated by moving pictures and hand-tinted lantern slides. Emery conducted most of the presentations. His first engagement was at the Gamut Club in Los Angeles. Before going on he suffered a severe bout of stage fright, complete with trembling knees and pounding heart.

The chairman, Mr. Blanchard, started the proceedings. "Ladies and gentlemen, I know you have all read in the papers of the Kolb brothers and their perilous journey through Grand Canyon. We have the honor of having with us tonight one of the brothers who will entertain you, and it gives me great pleasure to introduce to you Emery C. Kolb, who just came down the Arkansas River."

Emery rose to his feet with a smile and said, "Ladies and gentlemen, I know that Mr. Blanchard, being from Arkansas, does not wish to admit there is any other river but the Arkansas, but I must correct him to say ours was the Colorado."

The audience roared with laughter, and Emery forgot all about his stage fright. Turns out, he was a natural showman. He headed east to present the lectures and moving picture. Audiences responded enthusiastically, including such luminaries as Alexander Graham Bell, inventor of the telephone, and his son-in-law Gilbert Grosvenor, president of the National Geographic Society.

Grosvenor was so impressed that he arranged for Emery to present the program to the society in Washington, D.C., where it was attended by standing-room-only crowds. Even better for the brothers, the August 1914 issue of *National Geographic* devoted all but six pages to the Kolbs and the Grand Canyon.

Opposite: The huge chockstone wedged above Shinumo Canyon was a favorite tourist attraction. *Below:* The Kolbs' photo of the spot was used in *National Geographic* in 1914.

After Ellsworth rowed to the Gulf of California in the spring of 1913 in his $18 boat, he started writing a book. *Through the Grand Canyon from Wyoming to Mexico* would be released in 1914, complete with a foreword by Owen Wister that took some hard jabs at the Santa Fe Railway. Wister, who is best remembered for his 1902 novel *The Virginian*, widely regarded as the first Western and the blueprint for all cowboy novels that followed, questioned why the Harvey Company was trying to crush the independent brothers. Needless to say, Harvey officials weren't clamoring for signed copies of Ellsworth's book.

DUELING STUDIOS

Despite the efforts of the railroad to dislodge the Kolbs, the brothers were barnacled to the canyon wall. The Kolbs' river trip and subsequent lectures raised their profile so that many canyon visitors came looking for them, which makes the Harvey Company's next move seem especially ruthless.

They brought in their big gun, architect Mary Colter, and commissioned her to design a new building, one that would serve as a decoy studio. The Lookout, as it was originally called, opened in 1914. It rises in rubble stacks from the rim, looking very much like a dwelling of the Ancestral Puebloan tribes. Colter allowed the edge of the canyon to define the shape of the stone structure so it blends seamlessly with its surroundings.

That's very much a Colter trademark. She strived to create designs that appeared indigenous and organic. Irregularly fitted stones allowed soil to collect in the cracks, where plants have

Ellsworth Kolb was amiable, soft spoken, and absolutely fearless.

Through the GRAND CANYON from WYOMING to MEXICO
Ellsworth L. Kolb

EXPLORER AUTHOR

Ellsworth's book *Through the Grand Canyon from Wyoming to Mexico* was a hit. The heart-pounding adventure, blended with striking description and told in a straightforward style, caught on with the public. And like so much else, writing seemed to come naturally to Ellsworth.

On March 11, 1914, Ellsworth wrote to Blanche, "I just came from Mr. Wisters [sic] home. He has my manuscript and says he was sorry when it ended at Lees Ferry, which is as far as I have the finished copy. He gave me a lot of encouragement, and he made a few corrections. He says he will write a short introduction for it, and will write a letter to Macmillan, his publishers telling them what he thinks of it. Kind of encourages a fellow a little."

Released by Macmillan in 1914, the book went through twenty-seven reprintings, staying in circulation all the way through 1974. After being unavailable for over three decades, Grand Canyon Association, the nonprofit partner of Grand Canyon National Park, released a new edition that recaptures the original. The text was reproduced from digital scans, negatives of the photos were tracked down, and Owen Wister's foreword that the railroad found so objectionable is intact.

Beautiful Lookout Studio was built in a location meant to distract visitors away from Kolb Studio. *Below:* A Kolb brothers' sign near the mule corral, directing visitors to their studio.

taken root, making it difficult to tell where the building ends and the canyon begins.

The multilevel structure, now known as Lookout Studio, clings to the rim about 100 yards east of Kolb Studio. Telescopes were mounted inside, pointed toward the abyss. Paintings, postcards, and photographs were sold. So anyone venturing from Grand Canyon Village in search of the rimside photography studio they had heard about arrived first at the Harvey Company establishment. It was a fine bit of architectural misdirection.

To make matters worse, the Harvey Company built the mule corral directly in front of Kolb Studio, disrupting that path and making sure the family enjoyed a summer fragrance of Eau de Donkey.

Hopi House was the first freestanding building designed by Mary Colter. *Top:* Desert View Watchtower is perched on the eastern edge of Grand Canyon National Park. *Right:* Mary Colter, circa 1892.

BUILDING A LEGACY

Architect Mary Elizabeth Jane Colter was America's most influential female designer and revolutionized Southwest construction with her innovative use of local materials, her respect for native cultures, and a fierce sense of place.

Born in Pittsburgh (just like the Kolbs) in 1869, Colter lived in Texas, Colorado, and Minnesota before receiving her training at the California School of Design. Colter impressed the Harvey Company with her first assignment, an interior decorating job, and in 1904 was commissioned to design retail space at Grand Canyon. She built Hopi House, a gift shop and cultural center next to El Tovar Hotel. But while stately El Tovar borrows styles from Swiss chalets, Colter's structure looks as if it has perched there for centuries. The multiple stepped roofs give the impression of pueblo architecture, evocative of the Hopi dwellings of Oraibi.

Colter was hired permanently by the Harvey Company in 1910 and began putting her distinctive mark on the Grand Canyon. At the time, European ideas still held considerable sway over architectural styles in the United States. Colter pushed things in a drastically different direction with her use of site materials and efforts to create buildings harmonious with their natural setting. She laid out a blueprint for National Park Service structures. Her style became known as National Park Service rustic and can be seen in parks throughout the West.

Colter died in 1958. The bulk of Colter's surviving work can be found in Arizona, including the elegant La Posada Hotel in Winslow (1929) and many of the most notable Grand Canyon structures, such as Bright Angel Lodge (1935), Hopi House (1905), Lookout Studio (1914), Desert View Watchtower (1932), Hermits Rest (1914), and Phantom Ranch (1922).

Although the lecture tour proved to be successful, it also put a strain on the relationship between the brothers. During the winter of 1914, Ellsworth had pushed to expand the tour to include midwestern venues, even without a guaranteed fee. Emery opposed the idea at first but finally relented. In retrospect, scheduling January events in Cleveland, Ohio, smacks of poor planning. Blizzards have a way of thinning out crowds, and sure enough, the lectures were poorly attended.

It was during this rough patch that the Kolbs talked of going their separate ways. They would eventually reach an agreement to each work a two-year shift, with the brother at the studio paying rent to the other.

Things also got a little easier in 1915 when Ralph Cameron gave them permission to build an addition to the studio. They expanded their living quarters and, more important, built an auditorium that seated approximately seventy-five people and allowed them to show the movie of their river trip to Grand Canyon visitors.

That film would become a canyon institution. They showed the movie every day starting on April 15, 1915, and continued through 1976. Emery narrated it until 1932, when a recorded voice-over was added. Afterward, he continued to introduce the film in person. As he got along in years, one of his favorite stunts was to tell the audience that he was too old and feeble to narrate the movie, then would turn as if to start the projector and sprint up the stairs, taking them two at a time, much to everyone's astonishment. Those decades of racing up

Additions to Kolb Studio in 1915 included an auditorium.

Emery doing what he did best, captivating an audience with his film and his lecture.
Below: Cards advertising the daily showings of the Kolbs' film.

and down the Bright Angel Trail toting photos of mule riders built some sturdy leg muscles.

Emery showed the film until his death in 1976. It still holds the title of the longest continually running movie in U.S. history.

CHASING RAINBOWS

Even a place as immense and untamed as the Grand Canyon couldn't tether a couple of adventurers like the Kolbs. They wandered far afield on numerous occasions, although possibly for different reasons. Emery was always looking to expand their photography portfolio, and Ellsworth just seemed happiest traipsing across wild country.

Hopi tribal members watch the Snake Dance ceremony in 1913. *Opposite:* Ellsworth stands atop Rainbow Bridge near Glen Canyon. Lake Powell now laps at the base of the span when the water level is high.

In September 1913, the brothers traveled to the Hopi village of Walpi to take moving pictures of the Snake Dance. Also in attendance were Arizona governor George Hunt and former president Theodore Roosevelt, who spent a night at Kolb Studio during the trip.

When the dances were over, Emery and Ellsworth ventured across the Navajo Reservation to John Wetherill's remote trading post in Kayenta. From there they set out on horseback, accompanied by Wetherill, to find Rainbow Bridge.

They chose their traveling companion well because only four years earlier, Wetherill became the first white man to stand beneath the towering sandstone arch. The "rainbow turned to stone," which rises to a height of 290 feet, is hidden away amid the maze of canyons gouged from the Colorado Plateau.

This was one of the most remote corners of the country. Reaching Rainbow Bridge required a long trek across arid table-lands, navigating boulder-choked canyons and skirting slickrock ledges with plunging drop-offs. Yet it is a startling sight to round the final bend and behold the world's largest natural bridge. To-day Rainbow Bridge can be reached by a boat ride across Lake Powell followed by a short hike.

Away from civilization, the brothers were a great team, always watching out for each other and balancing their more extreme tendencies. They brought out the best in one another. Without Ellsworth, Emery would never have experienced a fraction of the adventures he enjoyed. And without Emery, the business would not have thrived, giving Ellsworth the means to go gallivanting off on his next adrenaline junket whenever he felt the urge.

But the business also exacerbated their differences in temperament and personality. Emery was a devoted family man who craved security. Ellsworth was a footloose rambler who yearned for his next challenge.

Just a few months after their Rainbow Bridge outing, they were shivering through a snowy Ohio lecture tour and talking about one buying out the other. Yet even during this rough patch, Ellsworth wrote to Blanche from Toledo:

> Don't think that Emery and I are quarreling. We were never getting along better. We simply can't see things in the same way. Emery gets to worrying, then I am affected

Emery, Edith, and Blanche along the Bright Angel Creek near Phantom Ranch.

by his attitude. He can't help it, neither can I. As soon as I am alone I am as carefree as ever, and happy whether I am making money or not as long as my health is good. That is all that matters. …

Although Ellsworth and Emery resolved their differences over the winter, they began to work separately and to spend less time together.

Ellsworth and friend enjoying the rim on horseback.

Ellsworth and Bert Loper try out two new boats. *Opposite:* Ellsworth filming the river atop a rock outcrop.

WATER AND AIR

I N 1916, Ellsworth set his sights on a trip through Black Canyon down the Gunnison River in Colorado. It no doubt appealed to him because it might be one of the few expeditions more treacherous than the one the boys took in 1911. As he wrote to John Shields, one of the men who would accompany him on the journey, "I do not accept anybodys [*sic*] statement regarding impassable places."

Unlike the Grand Canyon, which is wide, colorful, and stepped with terraces, Black Canyon is a dizzying gash of vertical rock. Sheer walls of dark stone rise hundreds, even thousands of feet above the roaring river. Yet the defile is so narrow, sunlight can only penetrate the lower depths for a few minutes each day.

Only a handful of men had navigated the Gunnison through Black Canyon, and those were on scientific forays. No

Sheer walls of dark gray stone rise nearly 3,000 feet above the turbulent Gunnison River, creating Black Canyon.
Left: Ellsworth was the first person to envision running the ferocious Gunnison River as a recreational outing.

one had ever considered tackling it as a recreational outing until Ellsworth showed up. The river drops steeply in a series of fierce rapids, most of which have to be run because the steep walls rise from the water's edge, leaving no room to portage or line boats.

It took Ellsworth three attempts over the better part of a year, with countless hardships for him and his companions. And his companions differed on each try because no one but Ellsworth would go back into those moody depths again.

Despite wrecked boats—including one that became so hopelessly wedged between rocks it had to be dynamited—and

A boat is blasted loose from the rocks with dynamite in Black Canyon. *Below:* Emery cuts a fine figure in his Signal Corps uniform.

numerous injuries such as a busted kneecap, Ellsworth paddled out of Black Canyon in the summer of 1917. Naturally, he shot moving pictures.

By 1917, Ellsworth became the first man to have run, and photographed, the Green, Colorado, Grand, and Gunnison Rivers. Emery was often described as the tenacious Kolb, but Ellsworth had that quality in spades as well. They just applied it to different obstacles.

When the United States waded into World War I, Ellsworth tried to enlist but was turned down due to his age. Obviously, none of the recruiters had ever gone down a river or climbed out of a canyon with the forty-one-year-old.

Emery served a brief stint in the Signal Corps, receiving his commission just weeks before the war ended on November 11, 1918. After the armistice, the National Geographic Society contacted Emery about a distant field trip. They needed a photographer to document the scorched terrain of the Valley of Ten Thousand Smokes, created by the eruption of Novarupta, near Mount Katmai, Alaska, the largest volcanic event of the twentieth century. Emery was in the field for five months.

Big changes came to the Grand Canyon in 1919. After eleven years as a national monument—and relentless attempts by Ralph Cameron to have that designation invalidated—Grand Canyon National Park was finally established by an act of Congress and signed into law by President Woodrow Wilson on February 26, 1919. It was America's sixteenth national park.

Ellsworth Kolb taking a winter swim at Glenwood Springs, Colorado. *Below:* Ellsworth and companion riding a trail in Grand Canyon.

AGE IS JUST A NUMBER

Ellsworth was likely not pleased after the military deemed him too old for service. While Emery bristled at any perceived slight, his older brother just quietly set out to overcome another challenge. According to William C. Suran, Grand Canyon historian and author, Ellsworth decided to enter a marathon in New York City after the army's snub. With just three days of training he joined a field of 1,200 runners. Ellsworth not only completed the 26.2-mile race, he finished in the top third of the field. Not bad for a geezer.

BACK TO CATARACT CANYON

Ten years after their "Big Trip," the Kolbs found themselves back on the Colorado. This time they started in Green River, Utah, where they shoved off in wooden boats as part of a 1921 joint effort between Southern California Edison Company and the U.S. Geological Survey (USGS). The expedition was surveying Cataract Canyon to aid in identifying potential dam sites.

William Chenoweth, the expedition leader, hired Ellsworth as head boatman. Emery was one of two photographers who were part of the group. Emery had patched up the *Edith* for the journey. He and the other photographer, Henry Rauch, rode in the *Edith*, giving them the opportunity to stop for photos without delaying the survey.

The USGS explored Cataract Canyon with Ellsworth serving as head boatman and Emery as photographer. *Right:* Members of the USGS surveyed Cataract Canyon in 1921.

Emery's primary reason for joining the expedition may have been to gather additional footage to supplement their movie, playing to packed houses at the studio auditorium on the South Rim. And it worked out. He filmed some exciting scenes during the only serious mishap.

Ellsworth attempted to run ferocious Dark Canyon Rapid only to maroon the boat on rocks about fifty feet from shore. The others threw him a line that he tied on, but despite their best efforts they couldn't pull the boat free. Ellsworth finally used the line to shinny across. Fortunately, since the boat held important maps and food, the watertight compartments held fast. The next day, using a crude pulley fashioned from driftwood, they were able to wrangle the boat loose.

By the summer of 1922, the government had surveyed all the canyons of the Colorado River except Marble and Grand.

Rescuing Ellsworth from a boat trapped in a Dark Canyon rapid on the USGS expedition. *Opposite:* Cataract Canyon.

HAPPY LANDINGS

The final Grand Canyon frontier was the airspace, considered by many to be as treacherous as the waterways. Due to updrafts and unpredictable air currents, aerial engineers had declared that landing a plane in the depths of the canyon would be extremely dangerous if not downright impossible. Not a good thing to say to Ellsworth, who probably regarded it as some kind of double-dog dare.

Ellsworth hired R. V. Thomas, a barnstorming WWI flyer and stunt pilot, and made arrangements to fly into the canyon. Ellsworth would ride along and act as cameraman. The two scouted a likely landing spot near Plateau Point, just beyond

Pilot R. V. Thomas and passenger and cameraman Ellsworth Kolb did what many
thought impossible and landed a plane in the Grand Canyon.

The first airplane flight into the Grand Canyon, with Ellsworth as a passenger, circles the rim before descending into the depths.

Indian Garden. They even obtained permission from the park superintendent.

On August 8, 1922, Thomas and Ellsworth took off from the small Williams airstrip. They followed the railroad tracks to the big chasm. People in the village cheered as the plane circled out over the canyon, testing the air, and then dropped below the rim.

After a few aerial acrobatics, Thomas pointed the little plane toward the landing spot, which suddenly seemed ridiculously abrupt. Just before setting it down, he advised Ellsworth to loosen his seat belt and be ready to jump out if necessary. Although not exactly what anyone wants to hear from the pilot, it all worked out. The plane touched down on a strip of land that park rangers had cleared and came bouncing to a stop several feet from the edge.

Cruel winds were blowing, so Thomas chocked the wheels and he and Ellsworth hoofed out on the Bright Angel Trail. Soon after reaching the top, they received word that a storm had swung the plane halfway around and broken the tail skid. Repairs were made the next morning with baling wire and an automobile spring, and Thomas took off, banked against the wind, and began circling to gain altitude until he cleared the rim.

The Fred Harvey Company hired Thomas to repeat the performance ten days later, but with a cameraman more to their liking, someone from Fox News. That newsreel was shown throughout the United States and later became part of the advertising campaign for the railroad and the Southwest. Ellsworth's role was soon forgotten.

SURVEYING THE GRAND

The 1923 USGS expedition to survey the Grand Canyon drew national attention. This was the last unmapped section of the Colorado River, one still shrouded in an aura of mystery and danger. The last two men to successfully navigate the length of the Grand Canyon by boat were brothers named Kolb.

Colonel Claude Birdseye headed up the expedition and was charged with making an unbroken level survey line through Marble and Grand Canyons and running the line up side canyons. After much back-and-forth negotiating, he hired Emery as head boatman. Most of the haggling between the two men centered on when and where Emery could take photographs and movies. Birdseye wanted nothing to interfere with the official purpose of the trip, and Emery assured him it wouldn't. But Emery also wanted some control over the film rights, since two other members of the crew were wielding cameras.

The expedition repaired three boats left at Lees Ferry by the 1921 Cataract Canyon expedition, brought in one new boat, and launched on August 1, 1923. A surprising addition to the usual river supplies was a battery-operated radio. No one knew what signals, if any, they would pick up within the depths of the canyon, but the radio performed admirably. Stations in Los Angeles, San Francisco, Salt Lake City, and Colorado Springs came in clearly at various times through the trip. From the bottom of the Grand Canyon, the survey party learned of the death of Pres-

Members of the USGS Birdseye expedition relax at Lees Ferry.

Claude Birdseye and Emery Kolb operate the USGS expedition radio in Marble Canyon. *Below:* Edith Kolb.

ident Warren Harding and heard the results of a World Series game. A land once so isolated was becoming less so.

The expedition rested on the day of the late president's funeral at a small rapid formed around a large boulder in the middle of the river. They named it President Harding Rapid.

When the expedition resupplied at the base of Hance Trail, sixteen-year-old Edith Kolb rode down with the mule string to see her father run a rapid. After Emery took the first boat through, Edith begged to try it. Emery said no, but of course, in the special language between father and daughter, no is just a slightly delayed yes.

With a life jacket cinched up tight, Edith was a passenger as one of the other boatmen (Emery was probably too nervous) plunged through Hance Rapid. Crashing waves soaked them both, but there were no other mishaps. Thus, on August 19, 1923, Edith Kolb became the first woman to run a Grand Canyon rapid.

Due to the high profile of the expedition, family, friends, and onlookers gathered to meet the men at the river wherever trails came down the canyon walls. One of those in attendance was a newsreel photographer, which again irked Emery, who believed he had an agreement for exclusive photo and movie rights. After multiple confrontations with Birdseye and the other crewmembers who were filming, Emery felt like he had been deceived. Tensions finally boiled over, and Emery quit the expedition at Hermit Rapid.

Blanche and Edith had traveled down Hermit Trail to visit

BRIDGE OVER TROUBLED WATERS

Running a rapid was not Edith Kolb's only Grand Canyon first. She achieved another while staying dry. Crossing the Colorado River deep in the canyon in the early days was a dicey proposition. It meant taking a boat across dangerous currents to the opposite shore with livestock swimming behind. In 1907, canyon pioneer Dave Rust installed a precarious cableway capable of ferrying across one mule at a time in a large metal cage strung across the river on a cable. The park service constructed a flimsy, swaying bridge near the foot of the Bright Angel Trail in 1921. A teenage Edith, astride a reluctant mule, became the first person to cross the span.

With visitation increasing in the park, it soon became necessary for infrastructure improvements. Trail repairs were followed by the construction of a new and sturdier steel suspension bridge. Mules hauled most of the 122 tons of materials needed. But the 550-foot-long suspension cables, each weighing a ton, had to be carried on the shoulders of forty-two Havasupai tribesmen down the steep and twisted South Kaibab Trail.

While building the bridge, men hung from slings above the river as they installed supports. Once completed in 1928, the Kaibab Bridge, better known as the Black Bridge, connected the South Rim to the North Rim. It is used by both hikers and mules. The nearby Silver Bridge was built in the late 1960s for hiker traffic but also supports the transcanyon water pipeline.

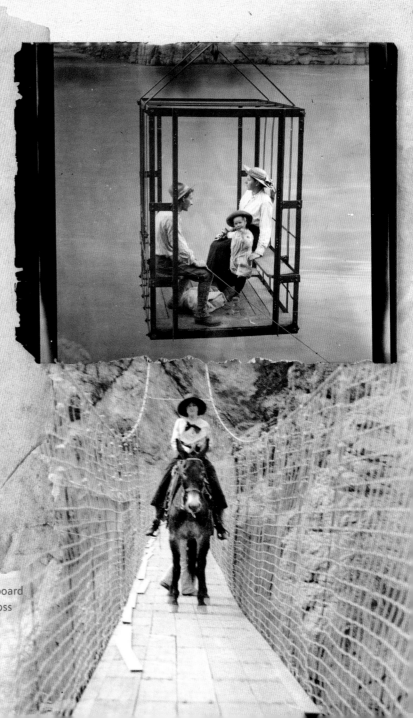

Top: Emery, Blanche, and Edith cross the Colorado River aboard Dave Rust's tramway. *Right:* Edith was the first person to cross the Kaibab suspension bridge when it opened in 1921.

Heavy afternoon thunderstorms can cause flash floods in the canyon.

the camp, and they were able to persuade Emery to continue. It proved to be a fortuitous decision.

On September 18, the men made camp in a cove below Lava Falls. Heavy rains had been a regular occurrence for much of the trip, and washes and creeks draining into the Colorado were running high. During the evening, the river rose and the turbulent water began banging the boats together. The men dragged the boats higher on the beach and had to drag them again an hour later until they were out of sand.

Middle Granite Gorge.

A member of the 1923 USGS expedition experiences the beauty of Muav Gorge above Havasu Creek. *Right:* Chef Felix Kominsky, helped by Elwyn Blake and Leigh Lint, added a gourmet touch to the meals on the expedition.

From his 1911 journey, Emery remembered a wide shelf of beach not far downriver. He and another boatman pushed off in the darkness. Hugging the shoreline they made their way to the landing spot. They clambered back over the rocks to find the little cove being submerged. Using a block and tackle, they pulled one boat up on a rock wall and quickly paddled the other two downstream.

It was mostly a sleepless night, with men in both camps struggling to keep the boats above the raging river, which finally crested the next day after rising twenty-one feet.

It took two days for the water to recede so the survey could continue. In the meantime, headlines were blaring around the country about the Grand Canyon flood and speculating on the fate of the expedition. Search planes were sent out, and it was a tense few days until Emery and the men arrived at Diamond Creek for their next resupply.

The surveyors completed their work on October 13. Birdseye would always credit Emery for saving lives and equipment. And the number of men who had successfully rowed the length of the Grand now numbered almost three dozen.

Emery and Ellsworth.
Opposite: Ellsworth's
photo of a woman
beneath a chockstone.

CHAPTER

SEARCHING FOR LOST LOVE

IT ALL CAME DOWN TO A COIN FLIP.
That's how the brothers decided who stayed at the canyon and who moved on. Their relationship felt like it was becoming unworkable in the winter of 1914, so they flipped for it. Best two out of three—heads, Emery would keep the studio; tails, Ellsworth would take over.

Emery flipped and it came up heads. Ellsworth flipped and it was heads. Ellsworth even flipped a third time, and it came up heads again. It was as if the Universe wanted to make it very clear who was supposed to stay and operate the studio.

Had things gone the other way, no Kolb Studio would

exist at the Grand Canyon. There likely would only be an empty space near the head of the Bright Angel Trail, and maybe a sign with a few photos remembering two brothers who once lived and worked there.

While Ellsworth never backed down from a challenge, he was far too easygoing and prone to restlessness. It's extremely unlikely he would have dug in and fought the long ongoing battles Emery did to keep the business viable. And he also didn't have someone like Blanche working alongside him. Blanche was in many ways the anchor that kept the little studio attached to the canyon wall.

Blanche ran the business by herself for months at a time while raising a child. Plus, she provided strength and encouragement for her husband, the man she called her own "bunch of garlic." He valued her calming influence. When Emery wrote to Blanche to tell her of the decision he and Ellsworth had reached about the business and the results of the coin flip, he closed this way:

> Personally I think I would have chosen to leave the canyon but it is now up to us. You & I will give us all a better chance to show what we can do. I of course will do nothing until hearing from my own dear wife for advise [*sic*]. You always know best dear.

Even with the decision made, the Kolb brothers stayed together for another decade, although they generally worked apart. Ultimately, when it came time for the final split, the

Blanche, Edith, and a friend below the rim.

brothers agreed—after protracted and sometimes bitter negotiations—that Ellsworth would receive $150 a month and Emery and his family would continue to live at the studio. In 1924, Ellsworth left the Grand Canyon and moved to Los Angeles. Their parents, Edward and Ella, had settled out there a few years earlier.

In 1925, Emery received permission from the National Park Service to expand the studio's auditorium to better handle the growing crowds. A darkroom and laboratory were also installed, with work finishing in 1926—the final additions to the building.

TAKEOFFS AND LANDINGS

Always a savvy entrepreneur, Emery realized the potential for sightseeing flights over the Grand Canyon early on. In 1925, he applied for a permit to use an old mining claim outside the national park as an airstrip. When the Forest Service granted his request, he cleared and graded the property and began mailing letters to airline operators.

Most companies weren't interested in what they perceived as a dangerous harebrained notion like repeatedly flying across an immense gully. But Emery did receive a letter from J. Parker Van Zandt and began a correspondence.

Van Zandt was chief pilot for Ford Motor Company's new airline division. When he delivered Ford's first all-metal Tri-Motor to its owner in California, Van Zandt got a glimpse of the Grand Canyon from the air. He convinced the head of the airline division, William Stout, that sightseeing canyon flights

Ellsworth enjoys Catalina Island in California.

The only documented landing at the Kolb Airfield, in 1926. *Opposite:* Ellsworth next to a biplane.

had tremendous possibilities. Stout gave the go-ahead and told Van Zandt to negotiate a deal.

So why isn't the Kolb name prominently displayed at Grand Canyon Airport? While Emery was negotiating in good faith, Van Zandt also reached out to the Harvey Company. He worked out a deal with them and secured a lease for land at the base of Red Butte to build an airport. Van Zandt formed Scenic Airways Inc. in 1927 with Stout and other financiers.

Van Zandt planned to expand the air tours into other national parks. He bought up farmland on the outskirts of Phoenix and built a hangar, landing strip, and offices for Scenic. But the stock market crash of 1929 hit him hard and forced Van Zandt to sell his airline and property. Yet both are still in business. Scenic Airways changed its name to Grand Canyon Airlines in 1930 and is believed to be the world's oldest air tour company

THE SKY ABOVE

Shortly after Charles Lindbergh completed his trans-Atlantic flight, he visited the airport at Red Butte. Amelia Earhart landed at Red Butte, where Ernest Tissot, chief mechanic for Grand Canyon Airlines, worked on her plane. Tissot later accompanied Earhart to Hawaii, where he prepared her plane as she became the first person to fly solo from Honolulu to Oakland, California.

On June 30, 1956, United Flight 218 and TWA Flight 2 disappeared over the Grand Canyon. A missing aircraft alert was issued. A scenic flight pilot remembered seeing smoke earlier and flew out to the eastern edge of the canyon, where he discovered the wreckage. The midair collision killed all 128 people aboard the planes and was the deadliest civilian aviation disaster in history to that point. The disaster led to the formation of the Federal Aviation Administration. The crash site was designated a National Historic Landmark in 2014.

in continuous operation. The little desert landing strip kept the name Van Zandt had given it. The city of Phoenix bought Sky Harbor and expanded it, and today Sky Harbor International Airport serves over 40 million passengers a year. Grand Canyon Airport is the fourth busiest airport in Arizona.

THE MISSING HONEYMOONERS

In 1928, the Kolbs became entangled in one of the Grand Canyon's most enduring mysteries. Newlyweds Glen and Bessie Hyde set out on a honeymoon voyage through the canyons of the Colorado River—a feat no woman had accomplished. Afterward, they hoped to be offered book deals, lecture tours, and even a spot on the vaudeville circuit. The couple became much more famous than they had bargained for.

Glen Rollin Hyde was a farmer from Twin Falls, Idaho, and a passionate outdoorsman. He had experience on the water, running the Salmon and Snake Rivers in Idaho. Bessie Louise Haley was an aspiring poet and artist. They met on a boat trip to Los Angeles, fell hard for one another, and were married on April 12, 1928. Glen was twenty-nine and his petite bride twenty-two.

Once the crops were harvested in the fall, the couple set out on their belated honeymoon. Glen built his own boat, a twenty-foot wooden sweep scow, the kind of craft suited for the rivers of Idaho. They put in at Green River, Utah, on October 20, 1928. Glen also hoped to establish a new speed record down the Colorado. They were loaded with provisions but chose not to pack life jackets.

Glen and Bessie Hyde, days before they disappeared.

Emery and the Army Air Corps pilot who located the Hydes' abandoned boat.

The big flat-bottomed scow passed through Labyrinth, Stillwater, and Cataract Canyons without serious incident. They made impressive time, and in mid-November landed at the foot of Bright Angel Trail. The couple hiked to the rim to resupply and meet Emery Kolb.

After swapping river tales, Emery snapped photographs of the couple. When he found they were traveling without life preservers, Emery insisted they take his old ones, but Glen refused. It seemed to Emery that Bessie was apprehensive about continuing. Taking note of Edith's new shoes, Bessie commented, "I wonder if I shall ever wear pretty shoes again."

When the honeymooners did not arrive in Needles in early December as planned, Glen's father, Rollin, initiated a search. Finally, a low-flying plane spotted the boat several miles below Diamond Creek on December 19. The plane went up again the next day with Emery as passenger, at the urging of Hyde, to best determine how to reach the scow.

Ellsworth wired from Los Angeles, offering his assistance, and Emery told his brother to meet him in Peach Springs. Emery set out by automobile from the South Rim with Hyde, Chief Ranger James Brooks, and park ranger Michael Harrison. Expecting to build a boat, Emery ordered a few supplies to be packed in. Ellsworth arrived by train and hiked in to the mouth of Diamond Creek.

As soon as word got out about the boat being found but not the honeymooners, the national media went on high alert. Emery received a telegram from Paramount News on December 20:

HAVE YOU ANY MOVIES AIRPLANE SEARCH COLORADO RIVER
ADVISE COLLECT

On December 28, the Associated Press wired:

WILL BE GLAD TO PAY YOU LIBERALLY FOR ANY PICTURES
FROM HYDE FILMS FOUND IN SCOW STOP APPRECIATE
HAVING SOME NEGATIVES RUSHED HERE IF GOOD ADVISE
US COLLECT

The Kolbs patched up an old boat and set off down the cold Colorado to search for the missing couple.

A line from the Hydes' scow was caught midriver on a submerged rock.

Once the searchers reached the river, they found the rotted ruins of an abandoned boat and shored it up with boards pulled from the floor of an old mining-camp tent. On a cold Christmas Eve, the Kolbs and Brooks set out in the leaky craft. They found the scow floating upright in the middle of the river with the contents undisturbed, a strangely haunting scene. The bowline was snagged on rocks below the surface, holding the craft suspended in the current. A few inches of water had seeped in, but there was no apparent damage to the hull.

THE UNUSUAL SUSPECTS

Legends have sprung up through the years regarding the missing honeymooners. On a commercial Grand Canyon rafting trip in 1971, an elderly woman claimed to be Bessie Hyde. She calmly explained over a campfire that she had stabbed her abusive husband to death and hiked out of the canyon to begin a new life. She later recanted her story. Speculation ran rampant when famed rafter Georgie Clark died in 1992 and many inexplicable documents were found among her possessions, including Glen and Bessie Hyde's marriage certificate, as well as a pistol. The certificate later appeared to be a copy, and no conclusive link could be found between Clark and Bessie Hyde. Even Emery was suspected of killing Glen, albeit posthumously, to help Bessie escape. After Emery's death in 1976, a male skeleton with a bullet hole in the skull was discovered in the Kolb garage.

When the disappearance of the Hydes was featured on the television show *Unsolved Mysteries* in 1987, it examined the possibility that the Kolb skeleton was Glen Hyde. A forensic pathologist made a reconstruction of the skull's facial features and determined the remains belonged to someone else.

Still the rumors persisted, and Emery's name was bandied about over many a riverside campfire. In 2008, investigators—aided by newly discovered photographs—concluded the skeleton was that of an unidentified man who committed suicide at Shoshone Point in 1933. How it ended up in Emery's garage is another one for *Unsolved Mysteries*. Emery did serve on county coroner's juries, so he may have acquired it that way.

A boat stored in the rafters of the Kolb garage contained a skeleton discovered after Emery's death. *Left:* Emery Kolb.

They salvaged the Hydes' belongings and counted forty-two notches carved in the gunwale, one for each day. Bessie's journal consisted mostly of a daily tally of rapids run. No entries were made after November 30.

Before releasing the scow, Ellsworth couldn't resist taking the cumbersome-looking beast through a small rapid. The scow was then turned loose and the men paddled for Spencer Creek, where others waited with food and horses. No trace of the Hydes has ever been found.

Mermaid Doll

Oh! Mama dear, please come!
My dolly must be drowned,
When I put her on the creek,
She sunk without a sound.

Wee Betty's eyes filled with tears,
Where could poor dolly be?
Perhaps she'd turned into a mermaid,
And drifted out to sea.

—BESSIE HALEY,
from her unpublished
collection of poems, 1926

Emery Kolb stands with rope and camera at the mouth of a cave. *Opposite:* Emery Carl Lehnert, circa 1932.

CHAPTER 7

ADVENTURES AND GRANDBABIES

POOR EMERY. His archnemesis was the Harvey Company, but number two on his enemies list had to be the National Park Service. So he must have been a bit perturbed when his only daughter married Carl Lehnert, an NPS ranger. Still, the heart wants what the heart wants. The couple eloped to Mexico. And despite early trepidation, the family quickly embraced Carl Lehnert. In 1928, Edith gave birth to a son, Emery Carl, who, not surprisingly, was doted on by his grandparents.

Following the stock market crash in 1929, business at the studio dropped off. Emery took advantage of the slow time to pursue another adventure with Ellsworth. The two went looking for the source of the tallest waterfall in the Grand Canyon.

CHASING CHEYAVA

In 1903, tourist guide William Beeson spotted what appeared to be a giant sheet of ice glistening on the distant canyon wall. When the brothers glassed the ice field with a telescope from their veranda, it turned out to be a massive waterfall spilling down the sheer wall.

Each brother made the arduous trek to upper Clear Creek Canyon to see the falls from below, with Ellsworth taking the first known photographs. After the USGS river trip of 1923, Colonel Claude Birdseye asked the Kolbs to name the cascade, and Ellsworth suggested *Cheyava*, allegedly a Hopi word meaning "intermittent river."

At times it may not be much more than a streak of wetness staining the canyon wall. But following a wet winter, as the snow melts on the North Rim, Cheyava Falls plunges 800 feet in a furious cascade.

In September of 1930, the Kolbs went looking for the source of the falls, a deep cave gouged into the canyon cliffs. This meant making an uncharted descent from the rim, 2,000 feet to the top of the Redwall, followed by a sheer drop of 200 feet to a thrust of stone below the cavern entrance. The Redwall Limestone is a prominent layer in the Grand Canyon sedimentary makeup that forms sheer vertical cliffs 500 to 800 feet high.

After spending the night in the North Rim forest, the brothers clambered down through a long gash in the Coconino Sandstone until a precipitous eighty-foot drop finally blocked them. After lowering cameras, food, and equipment by rope—which

Cheyava Falls.

pretty much committed them to continuing—they lassoed a fir tree growing twenty-five feet out from the edge. Then Ellsworth, in his mid-fifties, and new granddad Emery climbed hand over hand along the rope and shinnied down the tree.

At another point they had to slide a dead tree down the wall to use as a makeshift ladder. They continued down the cliff face until reaching the ledge above the cave. Here they realized they didn't have enough rope left to make the final descent. This would be a likely time for less-determined middle-aged men to throw in the towel. Instead, the Kolbs spent a chilly night on the ledge, made the long climb back to the rim for supplies, then climbed back down to spend another uncomfortable night. The next day they built a boom over the edge and attached pulleys to lower themselves into the cavern. They finished in late afternoon with a storm brewing. Since they were out of food and water, Ellsworth made a loop in the rope, took the canteen, and started over the side toward the flowing water 200 feet below.

Ellsworth was halfway down when the storm hit. The lashing rain quickly turned to "hail larger than hickory nuts," as Emery later said. Howling winds spun Ellsworth into a twisted tangle of wet ropes so that Emery was unable to raise or lower him. A rolling drumbeat of thunder echoed off the canyon walls, and the almost-incessant scorch of lightning lit up the skies. Fearing he'd be swept over the edge, Emery tied off the rope and sought what shelter he could find. Ellsworth dangled helplessly, bouncing off the canyon wall and hanging on for dear life.

When the storm finally passed, Ellsworth unwound the

Ellsworth uses found timbers to rig a makeshift pulley for the long descent to reach the source of Cheyava Falls.

ropes and Emery lowered him to the cavern. He filled the canteen, and then Emery hoisted him back in the darkness. They spent one more miserable night on the ledge before climbing out. The outing Emery thought would take a day and a half had lasted six days.

Naturally, Ellsworth returned a few weeks later. He had set out to explore a cave and was determined to do so. With Emery reluctant to spend much more time away from the studio, Ellsworth needed someone to handle the ropes. He enlisted Jay Ford of Kanab, Utah, "190 lbs. of bone and sinew, a good out of door man and a good man to travel with."

They followed much the same route down the cliff face. And as Ellsworth wrote Emery on November 1, 1930:

> I stayed in the cave alone over night while Jay went back to the Coconino fir tree camp where we left a bed. I carried wood in over the rocks back in the cave, where it was warm and with the work kept comfortable in my shirt sleeves. Put sacks over the dust and slept quite well after the work was done.

Ellsworth discovered the water flowing from an opening sixty feet high, spilling over huge boulders. Inside, an arching dome soared to a height of 150 feet. A lake stretched for 600 feet into the recess, with the ceiling tapering down to within two feet of the surface. Deep within the walls, Ellsworth heard the music of cascading water.

Emery reached the ledge above Cheyava Falls by working his way, hand over hand, across a precipice.

SUMMITING SHIVA

Advancements in technology left fewer worlds to conquer, but the Grand Canyon still held its share of secrets. In 1937, one scientist turned his attention to Shiva Temple, a broad-backed plateau that appears to be cut off from the North Rim. Dr. Harold Anthony of the American Museum of Natural History theorized that after thousands of years of isolation, things might have taken a weird evolutionary turn high atop the wooded summit. A new species was even possible, he surmised.

Just four years after the release of *King Kong*, such a story was too juicy to ignore. The national press quickly began speculating on what giant ape or savage dinosaur was likely to rule that exotic patch of forest.

Before he ever started, Anthony made two miscalculations. First, Shiva Temple is not quite as isolated as it seems. Second, he refused Emery Kolb's offer to act as guide. Emery did not take kindly to such a rebuff. So while Anthony was carefully choosing his team of scientists, mountain climbers, and support personnel for this historic first ascent, Emery scrambled to the top of Shiva. Twice.

A narrow saddle connects Shiva to the Kaibab Plateau, 1,300 feet below the summit. Emery set out with a young man who worked for him, Gordon Berger. After traveling to the North Rim, they navigated the treacherous spine of rock to the base of Shiva, where they were faced with 1,300 feet of a sheer stone wall. Yet it didn't take long for an old canyon man like Emery to puzzle out a route to the top following a long crack in

Clarence Dutton

THE GEOLOGIST POET

The formations of the Grand Canyon echo with the names of myths, legends, and gods. That's the legacy of Clarence Dutton, a geologist with the heart of a poet. Dutton was part of the Powell Survey of the 1870s, assigned the task of mapping and explaining the impossibly broken land of canyons and cliffs that comprise the Colorado Plateau.

Dutton published a series of books that not only laid the foundation for modern geology but also waxed lyrically over the beauty of the landscape. He saved his most passionate prose for the Grand Canyon, which he called "the sublimest thing on Earth."

So it seemed only natural that when he began naming landmarks he dipped into mythology and religions from around the world. It was a tradition often continued by explorers who followed. Thus the Grand Canyon is populated by buttes, spires, and mesas known as Shiva Temple, Vishnu Temple, Wotans Throne, Cheops Pyramid, Apollo Temple, and Tower of Ra.

Unmarked Pinal Point, on East Rim Drive, offers views of Jupiter, Venus, and Apollo Temples, all named for Roman gods.

the sandstone. They explored the woodlands crowning the mesa, where they found evidence of rabbit and deer but no thunder lizards or overgrown gorillas.

Since the museum party was to include a woman, Emery made a second climb. This time he was accompanied by his daughter, Edith, her friend Ruth Stephens, Berger, and his pal Ralph White. They made it to the top of Shiva, where they hoisted a flag made from burlap sacks and enjoyed a picnic. Since Emery didn't want to further antagonize the National Park Service—they were cooperating with the museum expedition—he kept his Shiva outings quiet, but rumors spread through Grand Canyon Village.

The scientists launched their attack on Shiva amid much fanfare. Their base camp near Tiyo Point swarmed with media. Regular updates were carried and stories filed via shortwave radios. Porters strung ropes along the saddle to Shiva, and from there a team of renowned mountaineers led the ascent to the summit. The success of the expedition was radioed around the world.

From a scientific standpoint, not much was gained. Anthony stayed atop Shiva for several days to document his findings, which were disappointing. The deer, rabbits, and squirrels of the "lost world" weren't noticeably different from their landlocked kin. Anthony's final report may be most notable for what it didn't include. There was no mention of his most shocking findings atop impregnable Shiva: empty tomato cans, film canisters, a tissue smeared with lipstick, and a burlap flag tied to an agave stalk.

Opposite: Before the scientific expedition made their perilous ascent on unassailable Shiva Temple, Emery led a group to the top for a picnic. From left to right are Edith Kolb, Gordon Berger, Ruth Stephens, and Ralph White.

ADDICTIVE FOAM OF WHITE WATER

Emery continued his pioneer ways, taking part in more "firsts" on the river. In 1938, Norman Nevills guided the first commercial trip down the Colorado River. For the journey, Nevills designed and built a new type of craft, the wide plywood cataract boat. Two of the passengers were Elzada Clover and Lois Jotter, botanists studying plant life in the canyons.

After the party stopped at the foot of Bright Angel Trail, they visited Kolb Studio and invited Emery to join them. Emery rode downriver, manning the oars through one rapid and entertaining around the campfires with stories and his prowess on the harmonica. He disembarked at Diamond Creek and returned home. At the end of the trip, Clover and Jotter had become the first women to traverse the entire river through the Grand Canyon.

Emery kept Americans on the edge of their seats in 1940, when Robert Ripley's *Believe It or Not!* decided to broadcast a radio show from the bottom of the Grand Canyon. Ripley's idea was to put his listeners in a boat plunging through the turbulent waters of the Colorado River. Emery would man the oars. Narrating the action was an amateur radio operator named Barry Goldwater.

Ripley introduced the segment from the veranda of El Tovar Hotel and cued Goldwater. The crew launched the boat into fast water, where it was buffeted by waves. Goldwater offered a blow-by-blow commentary as the roar of the rapids filled radios across the nation. Then, suddenly, everything went silent.

Finally, Ripley spoke. "Well, something has happened folks."

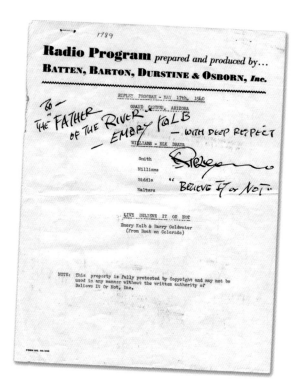

Emery's copy of the *Believe It or Not!* radio program signed by Robert Ripley.

Barry Goldwater broadcasting from a mile below the rim.

BARRY GOLDWATER

Born in Phoenix in 1909, when Arizona was still a territory, Barry Goldwater was a businessman and five-term U.S. senator. He was the Republican Party's nominee for president in 1964, losing to Lyndon Johnson.

Goldwater also maintained a lifelong love affair with the Grand Canyon. In the summer of 1940, shortly after his *Believe it or Not!* broadcast, he joined a Norman Nevills expedition and boated the length of the river, becoming the seventy-second person to raft the canyon. And he credited that trip with starting his career in politics. He traveled the state showing photographs and movies he took during the adventure, and discovered he enjoyed public speaking.

In 1951, while flying over the canyon, Goldwater spotted a natural bridge tucked high amid the cliffs near the head of Nankoweap Creek. He returned in 1954 as a senator and reached it from the ground. He petitioned the park service to name it after the Kolb brothers. Kolb Arch, with an estimated span of 147 feet, is the largest arch in the Grand Canyon.

The broadcast continued with ad-libbed commentary and Americans straining forward, listening for some indication that the two river runners were alive.

Several minutes passed until Emery could steer the boat to shore. Both men were drenched. Emery's skill kept the boat upright, but crashing waves had shorted out the radio equipment. Ripley finally informed listeners in a dramatic ratings-boosting reveal. The first broadcast from within the Grand Canyon could not have gone better.

Kolb Studio barely survived the early years of the Great Depression. They were beset with more tough times during World War II. Travel restrictions, shortages, and rationing sharply decreased the flow of traffic to the Grand Canyon. During the closing twelve months of the war, only 74,000 visitors entered the park. That changed abruptly when fighting stopped. By 1947, park visitation topped a half million for the first time ever.

They were better times but also changing times. More and more folks toted their own cameras. Color film was the coming thing. People were taking their own vacation slides, and Hollywood was cranking out slick productions of adventures, including canyon mule rides and white-water rafting. Sitting through a jumpy, flickering old black-and-white film held less appeal.

The NPS couldn't have agreed more. They had long considered the business unnecessary and the lecture a relic from a different era. Pioneers don't usually hang around so long. Since the canyon had become a national park, the Kolbs had operat-

Soldiers from the 51st Armored Infantry on leave take a mule ride at the canyon, April 1943.

Soldiers of the 7th Armored Division strike
a rimside pose, April 1943.

ed under ten-year leases. Starting in the 1950s, due to Emery's advancing years, the contracts were shortened to five years and negotiations toughened as the park service sought ways to squeeze him out. Or at least force him to give up and quit.

Which begs the question, had anyone in the park service ever met Emery Kolb?

The *Edith* was put on display at the park's visitor center in 1959. *Opposite:* Emery, 1965.

CHAPTER
8

A LEGACY PRESERVED

MERY HIT SOME MAJOR MILESTONES in the 1950s. In 1952, he marked his fiftieth year at Grand Canyon. That's a lot of trails hiked, a lot of rapids run, and many a smiling mule photographed. A stream of letters and telegrams poured in from friends and well-wishers across the country offering congratulations. The park superintendent kindly threw a big shindig in his honor in the Grand Canyon Village. Quite likely there were a few nervous stomachs when Emery took to the podium for his speech. But for an evening, old feuds were forgotten.

Just three years later, Emery and Blanche celebrated their fiftieth wedding anniversary. Blanche is very much the unsung hero of Kolb Studio. She kept the books and maintained the business during Emery's river trips, lecture tours, and other absences. As abrasive as Emery could be, Blanche was just as gracious. She ironed out many of the problems created by her husband's feisty temperament. She was a charming hostess, quick to throw a tea party or to organize a bridge game, and she was beloved throughout the Grand Canyon community.

When the brothers dissolved their partnership in 1924, they divided up the lecture circuit, with Emery taking the eastern portion of the country and Ellsworth taking the western half. Ellsworth gave a few lectures early on but never developed a passion for it. Even though he still had a highly regarded book he could promote, talking about adventures seemed far less intriguing than engaging in them.

Blanche and Emery Kolb on the occasion of their fiftieth wedding anniversary.

Ellsworth married in Seattle in 1924, but the union was short-lived. He took up drawing and painting and continued to receive the $150 monthly checks for his share of the studio. When World War II broke out, he took a job as a machinist at Douglas Aircraft. In 1946, knowing the studio had suffered hard times during the war, Ellsworth signed over all the royalties of his book *Through the Grand Canyon from Wyoming to Mexico* to Emery.

HARD GOOD-BYES

Accidents and illnesses began to slow Ellsworth down during the 1950s. He landed in the hospital more than once and dealt with high blood pressure and kidney problems. He also fell off

Ellsworth and Emery Kolb together
again at the Grand Canyon.

a ladder while painting his house. As someone
who had taken untold risks climbing to inaccessible spots in the Grand Canyon, he probably appreciated the irony that a tumble from a
ladder would lay him up.

Ellsworth died in his sleep on January 9,
1960, at the age of eighty-three. The family buried him in the Grand Canyon Pioneer Cemetery on a bleak winter day. He was an extraordi-
nary man whose accomplishments should have
perhaps drawn more attention. Yet that quiet
passing seemed appropriate. Ellsworth was
content to live far away from the spotlight—but
he lived well, with purpose and intensity.

Ellsworth never caught that freighter to China back in 1901,
but he had a zesty, rollicking, astonishing journey just the same.

Things would only get worse for the Kolb family in 1960.
On October 11, Blanche complained of pains in her chest.
When longtime employee Thelma Self came to her aid, Blanche
grasped her hand and then quietly, she was gone.

Emery, the old river runner, was suddenly adrift.

Even without his beloved Blanche at his side, Emery had
to press on. He was still personally photographing mule riders twice a day, developing the film, and printing copies. And
even though his lecture had been recorded since 1932, he still
introduced it to every audience. No doubt that's what kept the
crowds packing the auditorium, the chance to meet the last of

the Grand Canyon pioneers.

In 1962, the National Park Service upped the ante with a new contract that reduced the franchise period to three years and stated the studio would become the property of the park when Emery died. Since they had made their position regarding Kolb Studio abundantly clear, Emery knew they weren't planning to slap on a coat of paint, restock the inventory, and add more lecture showings.

This was the end. Emery's life's work would be gone. The NPS was going to do what the Forest Service, the Santa Fe Railway, and the Fred Harvey Company had long dreamed of doing. They were going to scrape that shambling studio off the canyon wall. And they could fire up the bulldozer soon after the eulogies were finished.

Emery argued against it, even reaching out to influential friends to speak on his behalf. Senator Carl Hayden, who had defeated Ralph Cameron in 1926, got the park service to extend the contract from three years to five, but the Department of the Interior was unyielding on the death clause. They didn't want that building cluttering up the rim of their canyon. Emery had always hoped to leave the business to his daughter and grandson to operate, but they had no desire to take it over. With no other recourse, Emery sold the studio he and his brother had started to the National Park Service in 1962 for $65,000 and the right to continue operating it until his death.

Then Emery set out to live to be 100.

Emery joins two of his great-grandchildren in a playpen for this 1961 Christmas card photo.

Two early river runners, Emery Kolb (left) and Frederick Dellenbaugh, at the John Wesley Powell Memorial on the South Rim. Dellenbaugh accompanied Powell as artist and assistant mapmaker on his second expedition.

Emery, circa 1967.

The centennial of John Wesley Powell's trip through the canyons of the Colorado River led to multiple celebrations in 1969. Emery traveled to Page, Arizona, for the opening of the Powell Museum. Afterward, a few river rats, including eighty-eight-year-old Emery, piled in a rubber raft at the foot of Glen Canyon Dam and made a fast trip down to Lees Ferry.

Returning to the Grand Canyon, the Powell Memorial was rededicated and a banquet given at El Tovar Hotel, with Emery as the guest of honor. He was introduced with glowing praise from Arizona Governor Jack Williams.

Emery would revisit the river in 1974, running rapids again at the age of ninety-three. A group of Colorado River historians were making the 280-mile run from Lees Ferry to Lake Mead. Emery was one of the special guest passengers for part of the journey, along with eighty-year-old Otis "Dock" Marston, an early Grand Canyon river runner who was compiling a comprehensive historical guide to the river.

Although Emery and Marston had known each other for many years, they did not get along. And since Marston also tended to be outspoken, the only thing noisier than the roar of the rapids were the arguments of the two elder statesmen. If age mellowed Emery at all, it was sometimes too subtle to notice.

Emery's final trip to the inner canyon was a touching one. An invitation was extended from the management of Amfac, the company that purchased the Fred Harvey Company in 1968. Emery had outlasted the powerful corporation. The new operators of the Grand Canyon lodges held a dinner in Emery's honor at Phantom Ranch and flew him and Edith down by helicopter. Emery presented the lodge with a selection of his photographs and spent the night in one of the cabins. Amfac was renamed Xanterra Parks & Resorts in 2002.

Commemorations became a pastime for Emery. Communities, civic organizations, and universities all stepped up to honor him and celebrate his long list of accomplishments. Emery became a speech-making machine and found himself accepting praise and expressing gratitude. Maybe age had mellowed him after all.

At the studio, his short introductions to the film were met with enthusiastic applause. Occasionally, he would forgo the recording and narrate the movie, just like in the old days. He never lost his love of performing.

Emery Kolb runs the rapids of the Colorado River one last time, at the age of ninety-three.

Skeleton found in the Grand Canyon in 1906, possibly a prospector. His pockets contained a Los Angeles newspaper dated 1900.

Toward the end of 1976, Emery suffered some minor heart attacks. He ended up in the hospital in Flagstaff after one. For a time he seemed to be on the mend, but then he contracted pneumonia. Emery Kolb died December 11, 1976. He was ninety-five.

When Emery was born, the Apache Wars still raged across the Arizona Territory. The Earps and Doc Holliday had not yet shot it out with the Clantons and McLaurys in a vacant lot near the O.K. Corral in Tombstone. He lived long enough to witness every Apollo moon landing.

The discovery of the skeleton tucked away in a canvas boat stored in the rafters of Emery's garage caused quite a stir. It's likely Emery knew that it would. The skull with a bullet hole ramped up speculation that these were the remains of Glen Hyde and prompted the *Unsolved Mysteries* episode a few years later. Emery always liked having the last laugh.

Emery was laid to rest in the Pioneer Cemetery next to Blanche and just down the way from Ellsworth. Emery didn't live to be 100, but he also knew he had won. The passage of the National Historic Preservation Act in 1966 changed things. It stated that historically significant buildings within the national parks that were at least fifty years old were afforded some protection.

Emery knew that the early sections of the building were safe, but the last additions, made in 1926, were still an issue. In a 1975 PBS interview conducted in the studio, he talked about it.

"This one is much over fifty years in the front part. This part right here is just over forty-nine years old. So I have another year to live to hold the studio."

As anyone whoever butted heads with him can attest, never bet against the tenacity of Emery Kolb. He made it by two months, and the entirety of the studio was protected. The National Park Service owned the building, but they couldn't tear it down. Emery had fought the railroad, corporate America, and the federal government—and won out. An enormous piece of Grand Canyon history was preserved thanks to an unyielding terrier of a man.

A STUDIO SURVIVES

Someone walking past Kolb Studio might immediately think, "Wow! It looks like Mary Colter was drunk."

Colter, the brilliant architect, put her unmistakable stamp on the Grand Canyon, designing buildings that blended effortlessly with their setting. Then there's Kolb Studio, designed by the brothers: a shambling by-the-seat-of-the-pants abode—a cabin that sprawled, a bungalow that exploded.

Now that the National Park Service had the studio, it became a matter of what to do with it. For over a decade, the answer was absolutely nothing. The building sat empty. The elements and local critters took a toll. Rodents set up housekeeping, birds nested in the upper stories, and pipes burst during winter freezes.

Finally, things changed for the better. By then there had been a generational shift at the NPS. Officials, recognizing the Kolbs' contribution to the Grand Canyon, began to see the studio not as an eyesore but as an asset. In 1990, the Grand Canyon Natural History Association (which changed its name to the Grand

Bright Angel Trail's steep switchbacks zigzag down the canyon wall. Kolb Studio is visible just below the rim.

Kolb Studio today.

Canyon Association in 1994), a nonprofit partner of the park service, supplied funding to launch a lengthy and complicated rehabilitation process.

First things first—the building was anchored a bit more snuggly to the cliff. Structural beams were repaired and replaced. The entryway was rebuilt. Log and shingle sidings were replaced. Old acrylic paint was stripped and a fresh coat applied. More than eighty windows were removed and reglazed in a painstaking process. Four balconies were taken apart and rebuilt. Retaining walls were shored up.

The association reopened Kolb Studio as a retail shop and exhibit hall, even as work continued on the large portion of the structure that served as residence for the family. The building encompasses 8,000 square feet spread over five stories and twenty-three rooms.

The work inside was equally extensive. The floors were repaired and refinished, and walls were painted. The living quarters were returned to a past era. Many original pieces of furniture from the Kolb family are still there. Other furnishings from the 1920s and 1930s complete the decor.

The Kolbs' film reels.

COME INTO MY PARLOR

Kolb Studio is open to the public as a retail store, with sales supporting the upkeep and maintenance of the studio. The Grand Canyon Association hosts exhibits and art shows in the auditorium where the brothers once screened the moving picture of their river trip. Unveiled in 2012, *The Amazing Kolb Brothers: A Grand Life at Grand Canyon* fills the space half the year. The exhibit includes a portion of the original film, artifacts, and many images.

The National Park Service occasionally offers limited tours of the residence. The tours start in the auditorium and then lead through the Kolbs' living quarters. Visitors will see the living room, dining room, parlor, bedrooms, the photography workshop and darkroom, and the greatest front porch on the planet.

PHOTOS © RICHARD MAACK

The Kolb family residence was refurbished with period furniture in 1998 that reflects Blanche's taste for thick Oriental rugs and carved pieces. The downstairs parlor is shown at right and lower right. *Below:* Blanche often hosted guests for bridge games and tea in the parlor on the auditorium level. *Opposite far left:* A cozy reading nook overlooks one of the studio's balconies.

PHOTOS © RICHARD MAACK

FAMILY MATTERS

Edward Payson Kolb was the second oldest brother, born February 19, 1879. He married Galena McClure, and they had a daughter named Helen. He was a railroad worker who died in Laramie, Wyoming, in 1953. He seemed to have had little contact with the family as an adult.

Edith Bell, sister to the Kolb brothers, was born October 21, 1890, but died the following month. She was the namesake of Emery and Blanche's daughter.

Ernest Vernon Kolb was the last of the brothers, born October 13, 1891. He married Agnes Cooper, and they had a son, Robert, who fought with the infantry in World War II, winning the Silver Star, Bronze Star with Valor, and numerous other citations. He also served in the Korean War as an artillery spotter, retiring as a lieutenant colonel. After Agnes passed away, Ernest married again, to Martha Norene Wilson. Ernest developed photos for Ellsworth and Emery and then worked for them in the studio during their river trip. He was a pharmacist's mate in the U.S. Navy and later sold pharmaceuticals on the road. He died in 1987 in Carson City, Nevada, at the age of ninety-five, just like Emery.

Emery "Smoky" Lehnert, Edith Kolb Lehnert's son, married Lillian Ruth Miller, who was also a teacher for over thirty years. They had two children, William in 1959 and Jennifer in 1961. William and Jennifer made frequent visits to see their great-grandfather Emery at the canyon. Smoky passed away in June 2012, just months after being the honored guest at the unveiling of the Kolb brothers exhibit.

Above: Three generations celebrate Christmas at Kolb Studio (left to right): Emery Carl Lehnert, Emery and Blanche Kolb, and Carl and Edith Lehnert. *Left*: Edith looks over the edge, with parents at the ready.

Edith at home with her dog.

BURYING THE HATCHET

Edith grew up at the studio, and she was an explorer while still in diapers, accompanying Emery and Blanche on many trips deep into the canyon. She was the first woman to run a Grand Canyon rapid, one of the first two women to climb Shiva Temple, and the first person to cross a bridge over the Colorado River in Grand Canyon.

Yet Edith never felt the urge to maintain the family business. Her husband, Carl Lehnert, continued to work for the NPS, and the couple traveled from park to park until 1959, when Carl was promoted to a post in Washington, D.C. Carl died in 1962, and Edith moved to Sedona, Arizona, located a couple of hours away from the Grand Canyon, the following year. Edith died in 1978, less than two years after Emery's passing.

It was the next generation of Kolbs who got to experience the final settling of old animosities. Edith and Carl's only son, Emery Carl Lehnert (called Sonny as a youngster and Smoky later in life) followed in his father's footsteps. After serving in the armed forces during the Korean War, he worked for the National Park Service for thirty-five years as a ranger and naturalist before becoming a biology teacher.

In January 2012, Smoky was honored by the Grand Canyon Association and National Park Service during the opening of a new exhibit at Kolb Studio dedicated to his family's contribution to the Grand Canyon. It marked Smoky's first visit since 1976, and this time he and his family—along with Ernest's grandson Steve and his wife—were feted like Grand Canyon royalty. Somewhere, Emery had to be smiling.

Ellsworth filming Shoshone Falls.

The brothers during the 1921 USGS expedition.

THE DEFIANT ONES

Ellsworth and Emery Kolb were the best ambassadors the Grand Canyon ever had. Period.

They weren't a government entity, a transportation hub, or a big corporation. They were just a couple of young guys barely out of their teens who traveled across the country to land on the edge of this impossible cleft in the earth. Other pioneers were drawn to the canyon as well, but each came seeking only personal profit. Certainly the Kolbs were running a business, but that business, by its very nature, was to convey the beauty and majesty of the canyon.

The Kolbs preached the gospel of the Grand. They spread the word in a way no one else could. Their photos ended up in homes around the globe. Their books, lectures, and motion picture brought the world to the rim. They were the voice of the canyon. It's unfortunate that the U.S. Forest Service, National Park Service, Santa Fe Railway, and Harvey Company didn't recognize that earlier.

The most remarkable thing about the Kolbs is the fact that they lived to be old men. They courted so much danger, it's a wonder that danger didn't sue for breach of promise.

And that studio? That monument to tenacity, that rambling, shambling collection of lumber and shingles that sprawls over the edge and slides down the canyon wall, somehow hanging on beyond the scope of logic and reason? The Grand Canyon—immense and epic as it is—would look positively barren without it.

PHOTO GALLERY

An early Grand Canyon entrepreneur, William Bass (right), talks with Havasupai Big Jim in Havasu Canyon. *Right:* Legendary Grand Canyon resident and tour guide John Hance on the rim of Grand Canyon, circa 1915. El Tovar Hotel can be seen in the distance.

The Kolbs often captured the proud elegance of Native people. *Above:* Hopi Ki Kopti poses for the camera at Kolb Studio. *Left:* Portrait of a Navajo man.

American orator, politician, and three-time presidential candidate William Jennings Bryan rides down the Bright Angel Trail circa 1904. *Left:* Many famous nineteenth-century Americans visited Grand Canyon and were photographed by the brothers, such as artist Thomas Moran, pictured here circa 1909.

President Herbert Hoover poses with Emery.
Right: President Franklin D. Roosevelt sits for a
photo op with a young admirer at Grand Canyon.

Walt Disney meets Emery and Ellsworth. *Left:* Writer and newscaster Lowell Thomas, known for making Lawrence of Arabia famous, with Emery, 1968.

Lord and Lady Halifax at Mather Point, 1944.

Albert Einstein (middle) with family and friends.
Left: The Apollo missions began in 1964, the same year these astronauts visited Grand Canyon and posed for a quintessential Kolb photo.

Navajo Bridge, which spans the Colorado River near Lees Ferry, is shown here at its dedication ceremony on June 14, 1929. Naturally, the Kolbs were present to capture the historic event on film.

The brothers also captured everyday scenes, such as this baseball game near the South Rim's recreation field, 1929.

As automobiles replaced horse-drawn conveyances, tourists flocked to Grand Canyon to see the sights.

Biplanes made their first appearance at the canyon in the 1920s.

The Atchison, Topeka & Santa Fe Railway built a spur line to the South Rim that was completed in 1901.
The Kolbs arrived on the train the next year. Here, train and station crew pose in front of the depot, circa 1915.

In 1919, C. J. Devine and Tony Pizzo, two discharged sailors, rode coast to coast on a promotional tour, literally handcuffed to their bicycles. The stopped at Grand Canyon long enough to pose for the Kolb brothers on the rim.

The romanticism of western scenes and figures was not lost on the Kolbs.

And then there were the less-likely portraits, such as this ballet class posing on a canyon precipice.

Scenic photos, such as these two images from the canyon's depths, were the brothers' stock in trade.

Showers drench the distant North Rim, with Garden Creek just below.

The Kolbs took hand-tinted lantern slides, like this one, on a traveling lecture series early in their photography career.

The Kolbs' sense of humor often showed up in their photos, as in this
self-referential shot of two mulish brothers taking snapshots on the rim.

ACKNOWLEDGMENTS

The author wishes to acknowledge the invaluable assistance of several people, most notably the members of Grand Canyon Association who worked so diligently to save and restore that shambling studio on the edge of the abyss. Very special thanks for the enthusiasm and talents of Lulu Santamaria, David Jenney, and Faith Marcovecchio. Also, the National Park Service accomplishes amazing things and has done so for a century, no matter what Emery sometimes said. Thanks to William Suran, now deceased, for his extensive research and writings, to Cline Library at Northern Arizona University for preserving the papers and photographs of the Kolbs, and to Richard Quartaroli for helping to create the remarkable exhibit at Kolb Studio and for so graciously sharing his files with me. Thanks always to Jill Cassidy for the endless opportunities she has given me to explore this beautiful state. And thanks to my wife Michele for everything. Absolutely everything.

And finally, thank you to Ellsworth and Emery Kolb, whose courage, tenacity, and artistic vision are a constant source of inspiration.

ABOUT THE AUTHOR

ROGER NAYLOR is a travel writer who hates to travel— at least anywhere beyond the Southwest. He specializes in lonely hiking trails, twisting back roads, diners with burgers sizzling on the grill, small towns, ghost towns, and pie. His work has appeared in the *Arizona Republic*, *USA Today*, *Go Escape*, *Arizona Highways*, *Western Art & Architecture*, and *Route 66 Magazine*. He is a senior writer for the *Bob and Tom Show*, a nationally syndicated radio program. He is the author of *Boots and Burgers: An Arizona Handbook for Hungry Hikers*, *Death Valley: Hottest Place on Earth*, and *Arizona Kicks on Route 66*.

For more information, visit www.rogernaylor.com.

PHOTOGRAPHY CREDITS

Courtesy of Northern Arizona University Cline Library, Kolb Collection, image numbers as follows:

cover: NAU.109992; p. iii: NAU.PH.568.75; p. vi: NAU.PH.568.3836; p. 1: NAU.PH. 568.10497; p. 3 (top): NAU.PH.568.367; p. 4: NAU. PH.568.3903 p. 5: NAU.PH.568.3501; p. 6: NAU.PH.568.3492; p. 8: NAU.PH.568.3730; p. 9: NAU.PH.568.230; p. 10: NAU.PH.568.3720; p. 11: NAU.PH.568.6380; p. 12: NAU.PH.568.8175; p. 13: NAU. PH.568.8683; p. 14 (left): NAU.PH.665.61; p. 15: NAU.PH.568.8387; p. 16: NAU.PH.568.3504; p. 18 (left): NAU.PH.568.5625; p. 19: NAU. PH.568.6947; p. 20 (left): NAU.PH.568.2786; p. 24: NAU.PH.568.1216; p. 26: NAU.PH.568.401; p. 29: NAU.PH.568.9151; p. 30: NAU. PH.568.3056; p. 31: NAU.PH.568.6716; p. 33: NAU.PH.568.8822; p. 34 (right): NAU.PH.568.3183; p. 35 (left): NAU.PH.568.8851; p. 36: NAU. PH.568.1075; p. 37: NAU.PH.568.846; p. 38: NAU.PH.568.278; p. 39: NAU.PH.98673; p. 42: NAU.PH.568.1091; p. 43: NAU.PH.568.3434; p. 44 (left): NAU.PH.568.9317; p. 44 (right): NAU.PH.568.1112; p. 46 (left): NAU.PH.568.9627; p. 46 (right): NAU.PH. 568.5734; p. 47: NAU. PH.568.10963; p. 48: NAU.PH.568.5765; p. 50 (left): NAU.PH.568.3686; p. 50 (right): NAU.PH.568.5809; p. 52 (left): NAU.PH.568.5270; p. 55: NAU.PH.568.9027; p. 57: NAU.PH.568.6745; p. 58: NAU.PH.568.3437; p. 59 (top): NAU.PH.568.3832; p. 59 (bottom): NAU.PH.568.2991; p. 60: NAU.PH.568.3750; p. 61: NAU.PH.568.3601; p. 62: NAU. PH.568.9000; p. 65: NAU.PH.568.8819; p. 67: NAU.PH.568.3518; p. 70: NAU.PH.568.4708; p. 71: NAU.PH.568.2791; p. 72: NAU.PH.568.1680; p. 73: NAU.PH.568.46922; p. 74: NAU.PH.568.386; p. 75: NAU. PH.568.241; p. 76: NAU.PH.568.3877; p. 78 (left): NAU.PH.568.3722; p. 78 (right): NAU.PH.568.3722; p. 79 (top): NAU.PH.568.3742; p. 79 (bottom): NAU.108455; p. 80 (left): NAU.PH.568.243; p. 80 (right): NAU.PH.568.3175; p. 81 (right): NAU.PH.568.5365; p. 82: NAU. PH.568.5330; p. 83: NAU.PH.568.2742; p. 85: NAU.PH.568.4752; p. 86: NAU.PH.568.3597; p. 87 (top): NAU.PH.568.3581; p. 87 (bottom): NAU.PH.568.802; p. 88 (top): NAU.PH.568.322; p. 88 (bottom): NAU. PH.568.157; p. 90: NAU.PH.568.4986; p. 91 (left): NAU.PH.568.3237; p. 91 (right): NAU.PH.568.3643; p. 92: NAU.109992; p. 94: NAU. PH.568.8644; p. 95: NAU.PH.568.237; p. 97: NAU.PH.568.6384; p. 98: NAU.PH.568.4035; p. 99: NAU.PH.568.3596; p. 100: NAU.PH.568.5384; p. 101: NAU.PH.568.5387; p. 104: NAU.PH.568.9299; p. 107: NAU. PH.568.6152; p. 108: NAU.PH.568.1591; p. 109: NAU.PH.568.10493; p. 111 (bottom): NAU.PH.568.6679; p. 113: NAU.PH.568.512; p. 115: NAU. PH.568.1207; p. 120: NAU.100768; p. 124: NAU.PH.568.10813; p. 126: NAU.PH.568.1203; p. 130 (top): NAU.PH.568.336; p. 130 (bottom): NAU. PH.568.4050; p. 131: NAU.PH.568.3100; p. 132: NAU.PH.568.8991; p. 133: NAU.PH.538.5354; p. 135 (left): NAU.PH.568.6324; p. 137 (left): NAU.PH.568.8232; p. 137 (right): NAU.PH.568.8172; p. 138 (right): NAU.PH.568.967; p. 140 (left): NAU.PH.568.8185; p. 140 (right): NAU. PH.568.2847; p. 142: NAU.PH.568.2234; p. 143: NAU.PH.568.6410; p. 146 (left): NAU.PH.568.2413; 146 (right): NAU.PH.568.1280 ; p. 147: NAU.PH.568.6990; p. 148: NAU.PH.568.6091; p. 149: NAU.PH.568.8856; p. 150: NAU.PH.568.8834; p. 151: NAU.PH.568.3625 ; back cover: NAU. PH.568.3437

Courtesy of Grand Canyon National Park Museum Collection, image numbers as follows:

p. 3 (bottom): 16030; p. 7: 07731; p. 14 (right): 30539; p. 17 (top left): 08117; p. 17 (bottom left): 07729; p. 18 (right): 15815; p. 20 (right): 05433; p. 21 (left): 10892; p. 21 (right): 05556; p. 22 (left): 05222; p. 22 (right): 05431; p. 23: 03611A; p. 25: 00438; p. 27: 16057; p. 28: 18350; p. 29 (right): 05546; p. 34 (left): 16255; p. 35 (right): 17189; p. 40: 17249; p. 45: 17171; p. 49: 17149; p. 51: 17154; p. 52 (right): 17165; p. 53: 17157; p. 54: 17158; p. 56: 05562; p. 63: 06553; p. 68 (right): 06151; p. 69 (top left): 17010B; p. 69 (bottom left): 09514; p. 69 (right): 16950; p. 71 (left): GRCA 58590; p. 77: 15754; p. 81 (left): 17195; p. 84: 05255A; p. 89: 06933A; p. 93: 10175; p. 96: 11040; p. 102 (left): 07727; p. 102 (right): 13626; p. 105: 06291; p. 116: 15252; p. 117: 15215; p. 118: 03425; p. 119: 15660; p. 121: 06555; p. 122: 06931; p. 123 (left): 05575; p. 123 (right): 05533; p. 125: 17199; p. 134 (left): 05544; p. 134 (right): 05534; p. 135 (right): 05547; p. 136 (left): 05549; p. 136 (right): 05564; p. 138 (left): 05205A; p. 139: 14257; p. 141 (top): 10536; p. 141 (bottom): 10554; p. 144: 07448; p. 145: 06843; p. 152: 16411

Courtesy of the National Park Service: p. ii; p. 68 (left); p. 127 (top)

Courtesy of the United States Geological Survey: p. 111 (top)

Courtesy of Adam Schallau: Cover (background)

Courtesy of David Jenney: p. iii (background); p. iv; p. v; p. 67 (bottom); p. 127 (bottom); p. 128 (left and right); p. 153

Courtesy of Richard Maack: p. 129 (all)